WICKSELL'S MONETARY THEORY

Also by Guglielmo Chiodi

NUCLEI ELEMENTARI DI TEORIA ECONOMICA
SOVRAPPIÙ E SFRUTTAMENTO CAPITALISTICO

Knut Wicksell has always been considered an economist belonging to the "marginalist" school. In particular, his contribution to monetary economics has been seen as being within the framework of the quantity theory of money.

The present work offers a different way of looking at Wicksell's contribution to monetary theory. This is done by focusing on the different meaning which Wicksell seems to have attributed to the notion of "equilibrium" inside his own framework. The traditional role attributed to that notion (either as a "convergence" point or as a "gravitation" point) is dismissed in favor of a much weaker one: a simple "reference" point. In this way the inflationary and deflationary processes are not seen as temporary or accidental "deviations" from a norm as they are no longer seen as responses to objective self-regulating mechanisms. Instead they are seen as phenomena through which the policy adopted by the monetary authoriy is able to produce irreversible effects on the "equilibrium" position.

Within this framework the attention is necessarily concentrated on the cyclical processes undertaken by the economy, without according any privilege to an analysis based only on "equilibrium". This interpretation of Wicksell's monetary theory is contrasted with the methodological approach of both the Classical economists as well as of some members of the Swedish School of economists.

For a note on the author, please see the back flap

Wicksell's Monetary Theory

Guglielmo Chiodi
Professor of Political Economy
University of Perugia, Italy

St. Martin's Press   New York

© Guglielmo Chiodi, 1991

All rights reserved. For information, write:
Scholarly and Reference Division,
St. Martin's Press, Inc., 175 Fifth Avenue,
New York, N.Y. 10010

First published in the United States of America in 1991

Printed in Hong Kong

ISBN 0-312-05369-X

Library of Congress Cataloging-in-Publication Data
Chiodi, Guglielmo, 1944–
[Teoria monetaria di Wicksell. English]
Wicksell's monetary theory/Guglielmo Chiodi.
p. cm.
Translation of: La teoria monetaria di Wicksell.
Includes bibliographical references (p.   ) and index.
ISBN 0-312-05369-X
1. Wicksell, Knut, 1851–1926.   2. Money.   3. Prices.   4. Interest.
I. Title.
HB116.5.W53C4513   1991
332.4′01—dc20   90-8932
                                                           CIP

To my parents

'Suppose', said Pinocchio, more bewildered than ever, 'that I buried my five gold pieces in that field, how many should I find there the next morning?'

'That's very easy to tell', replied the fox. 'It's a problem that can be solved on your fingers. Suppose every gold piece yields five hundred gold pieces; multiply five hundred by five, and the next morning you will find in your pocket two thousand five hundred shining gold pieces.'

'Oh, wonderful!' shouted Pinocchio, dancing for joy. 'When I have collected these gold pieces, I shall keep two thousand for myself, and I shall make a present of the other five hundred to both of you.'

'A present – to us?' exclaimed the fox, as if offended. 'God forbid!'

'God forbid!' repeated the cat.

'We do not work for gain,' said the fox, 'we do everything for other people.'

C. Collodi, *Pinocchio*, ch. 12.

Contents

Preface		viii
Introduction		ix
1	The Ricardian Legacy	1
2	The Theoretical Scheme	14
3	Wicksell's Elaboration: Some Preliminaries	39
4	Wicksell's Elaboration: The Making of the Scheme	48
5	The Orthodox Interpretation	62
6	A Critique of the Orthodox Interpretation	87
7	The Itinerary of Hicks	94
8	The Swedish School	104
Bibliography		122
Index of Names		128

Preface

This is the English version of a book already published in Italian under the same title (NIS, Rome, 1983). No change has been made with respect to the original work, save some corrections in the references appearing in Chapter 1 and the elimination of a mathematical appendix.

My greatest acknowledgement of indebtedness is to my friend Professor Kumaraswamy Velupillai, whose help and encouragement, the extent of which is not possible to describe in a few words, have been essential for the preparation of the present edition.

University of Perugia   GUGLIELMO CHIODI

Introduction

Dissecting the work of an author and analysing only one part of it is quite a hard task, and in the case of Wicksell (1851–1926) complex as well – his scientific production embraces different topics, not only relative to the field of 'economics'.[1]

Instead of summarising and anticipating the main conclusions of the present research, it will perhaps be of more interest to the reader to know the reasons for the choice of topic and of the course followed.

I was prompted to go deeply into the 'monetary' part of Wicksell some years ago by Sraffa's hermetic proposition according to which the rate of profits is 'susceptible of being determined from outside the system of production, in particular by the level of the money rates of interest' (Sraffa, 1960, p. 33).

Inquiring into the possibility of establishing a 'monetary' theory of distribution[2] meant, of course, reflecting on the foundations of the monetary theory as such.

On the other hand, if Sraffa's writings of 1925–6 can help in a historical-analytical wider understanding of 'production of commodities by means of commodities' in general, his 1932 essay could perhaps do the same, in particular as regards the content of the above quoted proposition. In the 1920s and 1930s, in fact, there seems to have been renewed interest in the field of monetary theory – witness Keynes's *Treatise on Money* (1930), von Hayek's *Prices and Production* (1931), Lindahl's *Studies in the Theory of Money and Capital* (1939) and Myrdal's *Monetary Equilibrium* (1939). The *Treatise* makes explicit reference to one of the first fundamental Wicksellian works (Wicksell, 1898b), whereas Hayek's book declares itself explicitly as an alternative to it. And Sraffa's 1932 essay offers a concise critique of von Hayek's work – which is its principal aim – as well as useful clarifications and suggestions for interpreting some crucial parts of Wicksell's work.

This framework was of great help to me in reconstructing the Wicksellian scheme, which had seemed to set the scene for theoretical reasoning in the monetary field and in which an *approximation* has been made by Wicksell himself to a 'monetary' theory of distribution.[3] Sraffa's 1932 essay had put itself as an essential point of reference in the reconstruction – although it obviously needed further extention.

In the course of the research, however, a problem, more methodological than analytical emerged. The economic literature in fact has almost always considered Wicksell as a neoclassical economist and therefore the 'return to the classic programme' which started in the 1960s seemed a contrast to the reconstruction I was going to make. However, a detour back to the classics, in particular towards Ricardo (from whom Wicksell himself started his inquiry) set in different terms the operation of that 'return': the research on Wicksell induced me to consider the usual distinction between classics and neoclassics as it has emerged from the debate on capital theory as quite restrictive. This is essentially due to the fact that Wicksell's monetary economy framework of reference did contain ideas which further developed would have been able to offer new elements to a critique of the dominant strand on economic theory. On the other hand, one cannot safely state – as will be shown further on – that the theoretical system of the classics had no influence at all on the latter theory, especially Ricardo's, for in such a system non-negligible elements exist which the subsequent tradition utilised within its own analysis.

Naturally, what has been said so far reflects itself in the structure given to the present work. The intention of the first few chapters is to offer the basic theoretical scheme of Wicksell relative to a monetary economy. In particular, in Chapter 1 I try to point out the supposed methodology of the Wicksellian inquiry as opposed to the Ricardian one as regards the monetary aspects of it. In the latter the notion of 'equilibrium' together with the analysis of the adjustment mechanisms constitutes the base of reference for an approach which will be typical of the neoclassical tradition. Wicksell's detachment from this kind of analysis should be made evident in Chapter 2, followed by two chapters (actually not essential to the main argument pursued) regarding the itinerary made by Wicksell.

Chapters 5–8 contain a critical evaluation of the interpretations of Wicksell's monetary theory, considered the most relevant for the purpose of the present work, from which it becomes clear that the Wicksellian attempt to break out of the methodological network made up of the neoclassical tradition has been hindered not only – as obviously one can expect – by that tradition but also, though with different intentions, by some economists of the Swedish School.

* * *

Introduction

I want here to express my gratitude to all those people who in different times and by different ways have helped and encouraged me in the course of the research. In particular I would like to thank: Kumaraswamy Velupillai, who was the first to draw my attention to Wicksell's 'monetary' aspects and with whom I have profitably been able to discuss some problems connected with Sraffa's works; Leonardo Ditta, who patiently pointed out to me mistakes and offered suggestions on some parts of the work in endless conversations; Maria Cristina Marcuzzo, who read with extreme care two versions of the manuscript giving me useful suggestions; Luca Meldolesi, who discussed with me some central parts of the work; Marcello Messori, for his innumerable critical remarks which induced me to perfect several points in the final version; Augusto Graziani and Serena Di Gaspare for having communicated to me in detail their impressions and remarks, due to which I was able to eliminate many improprieties; Sandro Vercelli, for his suggestions given in modifying substantially some parts of the final version. It goes without saying that the responsibility for the remaining errors as well as for the opinions expressed rests solely with the author.

Acknowledgements must be expressed to the Italian National Research Council (CNR) for financial support and the Swenska Institute for a scholarship, which made possible a visit to Lund University (Sweden). In this connection I must, of course, thank Professor Bjorn Thalberg for the facilities made available to me during my stay at Lund, and, again, Kumaraswamy Velupillai for having made it concretely possible. (Both of them gave me the opportunity of presenting a communication at the International Symposium on the theoretical contributions of Wicksell held in Frostavallen (Sweden) in 1977.)

Last but not least my greatest debt is to my wife Rita and my sons Lamberto and Pietro whose intangible contributions have been, as always, decisive for the completion of this work.

GUGLIELMO CHIODI

NOTES

1. A biography is supplied by T. Gårdlund (1958). A concise biography can be found in R. Frisch (1952, pp. 655–9) and E. Lindahl (ed.) (1969).
2. For a first attempt by the writer, see G. Chiodi (1978).
3. See, in particular, K. Wicksell (1898b, p. 302–4). A systematic approach in that direction is a different task to undertake.

1 The Ricardian Legacy

1.1

One of the most recurrent features of Wicksell's monetary theory cannot escape even the least careful reader: his 'schizophrenia' in treating the quantity theory of money, particularly the Ricardian monetary theory. As regards the former, in fact, he maintains on the one hand that 'indeed, it is the only one which attempts in some degree to provide a rational explanation' (Wicksell, 1898b, p. 50);[1] and that it is 'the only specific theory of the value of money which has been propounded, and perhaps the only one which can make any claim to real scientific importance' (1906, p. 141). On the other, Wicksell tones down those statements by saying '*under given conditions* the Quantity Theory is capable of being correct' (1898b, p. 38); and it is '*theoretically* valid so long as the assumption of *ceteris paribus*' holds (1898b, p. 42); and he goes so far as saying, at the same time, that it is based on 'assumptions that unfortunately have little relation to practice, and in some respect none whatever' (1898b, p. 41) and gives rise to 'too many objections, as pointed out by later writers, to be accepted without modification' (1898b, p. xxxiii). In addition:

> That a large and a small quantity of money *can* serve the same purposes of turnover if commodity prices rise or fall proportionately to the quantity is one thing. It is another thing to show why such a change of price must always follow a change in the quantity of money and to describe what happens. (Wicksell, 1906, p. 160)

Wicksell's attitude with respect to Ricardo follows a line of reasoning similar to that which he adopts with regard to the quantity theory.

Starting with the aim 'to push on in the footsteps of the great master' and pointing out that in the Ricardian writings on money 'we find a perfectly clear and exhaustive, logically coherent treatment of the subject which does not seem to leave room for doubt or dissenting opinion' (Wicksell, 1898a, p. 68) as to leave anybody convinced that 'this theory [quantity theory] is fundamentally sound and correct' (ibid), Wicksell with the same determination maintains 'as so often with Ricardo the theory was given too one-sided a character; it was too narrow, it was not immediately applicable to concrete reality' (ibid, pp. 68–9). Morever:

> In his zeal to provide a striking proof of a fundamentally self-evident thesis Ricardo advanced a vague and partially erroneous argument, which could not fail to exercise an unfavourable influence on the subsequent discussion of the subject. (Wicksell, 1906, pp. 181–2)

From this clear set of generic propositions quoted, the 'schizophrenia' referred to above seems quite evident. In what follows, however, I will try to show how and why that 'schizophrenia' should be considered only *apparent*, and why consequently Wicksell's attitude with respect to the quantity theory of money, and in particular Ricardo's position, turns out to be perfectly coherent.

The problem, then, essentially consists in putting forward *the extent to which* Wicksell accepted the classical ideas on money and *on what* he decidedly disagreed. An attempt will be made, in the following pages, to draw attention to the way Wicksell tries to contrast the quantity theory of money, especially on the basis of his critique of Ricardo – and that would hopefully provide sufficient indications for placing his monetary theory outside the framework and tradition of the quantity theory of money.

1.2

As is well known, according to the quantity theory, variations in the quantity of money produce *proportional* variations in the general price level. It is essentially here that money differs from the analogous characteristics of other commodities, whose exchange value rises or falls according to whether the respective quantities increase or decrease, but in general *not* in the same proportion.

In an economy whose circulating medium exclusively consists of coins or notes and in which every individual makes exchanges by means of money, an almost invariant cash balance would be sufficient to meet the needs of trade; moreover customary reference to that stable and uniform cash balance would assure the functioning of the proportionate mechanism. Thus, a level of price different from the previous one would immediately make cash balance insufficient, so that variations in demand or supply of commodities, or both, would restore the price level of before.

In this way the quantity theory goes beyond the simple truism of its identity; but at the same time the hypothesis on which it is built is responsible for its highly disputable general validity – to say the least.

It is necessary to distinguish two aspects of the Wicksellian critique of the quantity theory. One regards the 'realism' of its hypothesis by means of which the absence of generality (usually attributed to it) is put forward; the other one, far more important, regards the methodological approach in the field of monetary theory, developed by Wicksell especially in his critique of Ricardo. Let us consider these two aspects, in turn.

Wicksell (1898b, pp. 41–2) lists the essential 'defects' contained in the quantity theory:

(1) a 'completely individualistic system of holding cash balance', whereas in actual fact 'cash balances' have actually become an 'accounting magnitude' mere 'legal conception', a 'right' for the individual to draw cheques on his bank within no rigid limits given once and for all and for all equal;
(2) an almost invariant cash balance (i.e. a fixed velocity of circulation of money), whereas in practice it is subject to considerable changes;
(3) most commercial transactions are mediated by money, whereas in practice both money and *credit* enter those transactions in rather variable proportions according to circumstances;
(4) the quantity of money in circulation, and the part of it outside, are sharply distinguishable, whereas in practice this is not true, because the latter part comes in and out without any prefixed rule.

The content of the critique so far summarised implies that the *simple* formulation of the quantity theory of money leads to a *naive* reduction of reality. Thus, the pure theoretical set of statements is one thing; it is another when the latter is put in relation to the real facts characterising the economic system. As a matter of fact, the circumstances to which the quantity theory of money refers 'are some of the flimsiest and most intangible factors in the whole economics' (Wicksell, 1898b, p. 42).

This first part of the Wicksellian critique of the quantity theory (the second one will be taken into consideration presently when the Ricardian position will be examined) is centred on the lack of validity of the assumption that forms the basis of the quantity theory discussion.

Wicksell in another place, borrowing an example from Hume, writes:

> Hume's well-known fiction [Hume, 1963, p. 307] of our waking up one morning to find double the number of shillings and sovereigns in our pockets, whilst everything else remains unchanged, may seem quite appropriate, but suffers from the defect that it is not a simplification of reality – which is permissible – but relates to a purely paradoxical case, which in the nature of things never can occur. (Wicksell, 1906, p. 160)

The systematic introduction of bank credit to the public, moreover, deprives the notion of demand for, and supply of, money of any separate autonomy as well as of any definite meaning (Wicksell, 1906, pp. 143–4). In the limiting case – which Wicksell will take into consideration in his scheme – where the circulating money is *only* bank credit, the quantity theory of money would be without 'its very foundations' (Wicksell, 1898b, p. 76).[2] Wicksell admits, on the other hand, the progress made by the quantity theory with respect to the 'mercantilist' theory, especially for clarifying 'the purely formal or conventional character of the value of money' (ibid, p. 38). Granted his critiques of the former theory – as pointed out above – he defends at the same time the essential logical core *in relation* to those theories of money which aimed to be alternative to that theory, but that, according to Wicksell, fail in their purpose.

The alternatives are either simply superficial – and ultimately turn back to the quantity theory – or self-contradictory – containing logical slips in the reasoning (apart from the contradiction with the real facts).

The 'defence' of the quantity theory set up by Wicksell, then, must not be understood as such, but simply as a means of emphasising the poor value – as 'theories' – of all those attempts which unsuccessfully tried to overcome the limitations of the quantity theory. A brief discussion on these 'theories', as we shall see in a moment, will strengthen the Wicksellian defence mentioned above, whereas at the same time it will make evident the necessity for Wicksell to build up his own alternative monetary theory.

1.3

The 'theories' taken into consideration (cf. Wicksell, 1898a, pp. 68–73; 1898b, chs 4, 5; 1906, ch. 4, secs 3, 4, 5, 6) can be conveniently divided into two groups: the first finds 'money' the exclusive cause for variations in the purchasing power of the latter; the second, exclusively commodities or production. Both groups have two characteristics in common: (i) to choose only *one* side of the possible mechanisms; (ii) to put forward the subordinate character of the 'monetary' phenomena.

The first group is represented by the cost of production theory of money which, in line with the cost of production theory of commodities, singles out the cost of production of the metal as the crucial element determining the value of the medium of exchange in relation to goods. However, there is a time-lag between the moment in which a variation in the production of (e.g.) gold produces its effects through variations in money prices and the moment in which a variation in the production of commodities takes place such that an actual increase in the circulation of the metal is needed. The effect of the first variation is extremely slow, almost secular, due not least to the fact that a massive production of the metal would hardly succeed in influencing the entire stock of gold in the period under consideration. Much more suitable to the needs expressed by the continuous variations of production of goods would instead be the monetary and credit policy (put forward by the banking system through the usual instruments) which is able to make more elastic the quantity of the medium of exchange in the economy. If this were not so, Wicksell says, 'it would be impossible to explain the rapid rise in commodity prices which usually occurs in times of business prosperity and the even more violent setbacks in times of crisis' (Wicksell, 1906, p. 149). The velocity of circulation of money, which is the crucial element in the above reasoning, does not fit into the cost of production theory; on the contrary, it enters the picture simply as an automatic and self-regulating process, in the sense that 'it presupposes that merchants and bankers would quite passively submit to seeing their safes filled to overflowing when gold is plentiful, and exhausted when it is scarce, perhaps to the last sovereign, without taking any steps to restore the normal position' (ibid, p. 150).

No less subject to criticism, according to Wicksell, are those attempts aimed at offering an alternative explanation, with respect to the quantity theory, of the movements of the money value exchange based *uniquely* on circumstances referring to commodity production – mentioning no event regarding money (Wicksell, 1898b, ch. 5, pp. 46–50). For instance, taking the case of commodities produced at relatively lower costs than before (due to technical progress in *one or more* lines of production) there would follow – according to the theory considered – price reductions of all *other* commodities such as to lead to a *general* relatively lower price level (cf. Wicksell, 1898b, pp. 26–8, and ch. 3, pp. 25–8; 1906, sec. 5).[3]

The basic mistake contained in this sort of reasoning would consist, according to Wicksell, in the pure and simple extension to money prices of a mechanism valid in explaining only *relative* prices. Thus, if a commodity has a lower price due to an augmented supply, this would mean a price *increase* in all other commodities – *ceteris paribus* – hence nothing can be said *a priori* about the general money price level. On the other hand, from a quantity theory standpoint, one would attain the same results as those attained through the latter theory.

If it is true that one cannot accept the quantity theory as it stands, it is equally true that one cannot accept those theories which apparently seem alternative to it, because of their faulty logic and one-sidedness in explaining money prices, i.e. considering exclusively either the commodity or the monetary side.

1.4

Parallel to his critique of the quantity theory and of the theories 'alternative' to it, Wicksell makes a punctual and stringent analysis of Ricardo's monetary theory as well as of the theory advanced by Tooke. The first part of that analysis deserves particular attention in order to better evaluate the methodological and analytical position which characterises (and justifies at the same time) the scheme proposed by Wicksell – and in so doing we land on the second aspect of the Wicksellian critique mentioned in section 1.2.

One of the problems at the centre of Ricardo's attention (and subsequently Tooke's) was essentially related to the type of influence exercised by the credit bank to the public with respect to money prices. It is Wicksell himself who pointed out that there existed unanimity of opinion on the analogue influence exercised by the issue of credit by the State in the form of paper money, so that, for example, an excessive issue was always considered the cause of an increase in the money prices of commodities (Wicksell, 1906, pp. 169–70); quite different, thus, to the influence of credit banks. As is well known, the controversies that arose in this connection during the last century were split into two strands of thought known as the Currency School on the one hand and the Banking School on the other. It is not necessary here to recall the characteristics of both (cf. Viner, 1965, ch. 5; and Rist, 1940, ch. 5),[4] but one, in particular, will be recurrent in what follows.

This is concerned with the *power* attributed to the banks in their influence of money prices. The Currency School did believe them to retain an *unlimited* power in that respect, used with large discretion on every determinate circumstance; whereas the Banking School did not believe the banks had such power, but emphasised instead their passive role in the variations of the purchasing power of money. The main thesis of Ricardo – one of the most influential and inspiring men of the Currency School – is that an excessive issue of banknotes, exceeding the amount which preserves their value, is exactly equivalent – in so far as an increase in commodity prices is concerned – to an increase in the quantity of gold in circulation for a given economic system. As the quantity of banknotes increases, their value would decrease in the *same* proportion. Treating banknotes and gold on the same footing is maintained by reference to the *ultimate* destination of the two: both the quantity of banknotes issued as well as that of gold would be definitively lent, and for a merchant asking for a loan it would be the same thing as taking the loan partly from a private lender, partly from a bank *or* entirely from a bank at which previously a quantity of gold was deposited. 'The analogy,' Ricardo says decisively in reply to Bosanquet, 'seems to me to be complete, and not to admit of dispute' (Ricardo, 1951b, p. 217). (The same principle would apply in the case of unredeemable paper.)

Whatever the excess amount of banknotes or gold, this would be *completely* absorbed in the circulation due to the *proportional* depreciation which necessarily would follow. Excess amount of the circulating medium and depreciation are thus two facets of the same metal. In order to better clarify his thesis, Ricardo imagines the establishment of a bank on the same principles as the Central bank. He supposes, moreover, the circulation in the system to be wholly metallic and 'sufficient for the commerce of the country' (Ricardo, 1951b, p. 218). Two alternative cases are considered: an open economy and a closed economy (the world economy as a whole).

In the former case, an issue of banknotes would produce depreciation both of the circulating medium and of the metal. In accordance with his earlier discussions (ibid, p. 54) the precious metal (coined or uncoined) would leave the country in which it is now cheaper. Under these circumstances money 'would be demanded because it could be profitably exported, and not because it could not be absorbed in the circulation' (ibid, p. 218). In the second case (closed economy) due to the impossibility of exportation, an excess amount of banknotes simultaneously issued in each country could add to the already existing circulation (supposed adequate) with no opportunity for banknotes to return back to the issuing bank. If this is objected, then, says Ricardo, 'I appeal to experience, and ask for some explanation of the manner in which Bank notes were originally called into existence, and how they are permanently kept in circulation' (ibid, p. 219).

1.5

Wicksell's critique of Ricardo's thesis is of great importance – at least for the interpretation given here – especially from a *methodological* point of view.[5]

A discussion of that critique, therefore, has the advantage of serving as an introduction to the entire analysis of the theoretical scheme which will be examined in this work.

It could be useful to indicate, though in a synthetic way, that the whole argument is based on the following thesis: that part of the classical system – particularly that of Ricardo – that deals with monetary problems contains several elements which the subsequent neoclassical tradition[6] has been able to take as a reference point in order to lay the foundations and develop its own monetary theory. In contrast, Wicksell's contribution seems to indicate an analysis going towards a new direction, which, however, the subsequent literature – save some contributions, especially from the Scandinavian countries and the late writings of Hicks – almost ignored or cut off, thus reformulating Wicksell's monetary theory according to the rules set by the neoclassical tradition.

Let us then see how Wicksell constructs his critique of Ricardo. First of all it is pointed out that the precious metal does not necessarily enter the circulation through loans; as maintained often by Ricardo, the case of gold coming from America would refute that. In fact, gold enters the importing country in payment for commodities, and in this way it obviously causes an increase in the prices of commodities (Wicksell, 1906, pp. 177–8).

As regards the issue of banknotes and the question emphatically posited by Ricardo on how they could exist and be maintained in circulation, it is pointed out by Wicksell that an issue of them does not necessarily take place when the amount of them in circulation is adequate or in equilibrium; i.e., an issue of bank notes can, in general, take place from a disequilibrium situation.

Ricardo's assumption of constantly referring to a state of circulation as 'adequate' should be considered not exclusively as a simplifying hypothesis. On the contrary, it represents a *result* of the Ricardian analysis: the economic system does have automatic mechanisms in its functioning, explained from inside economic theory, which would assure the realisation of an ever-attainable 'normal' state of the economy.

A straight corollary of this is that any deviation from that state can only be considered transitory and short-lasting, which by no means can influence the long-term position of the system in any fundamental way whatsoever.

Ricardo's conception permeates all his discussions concerning a monetary economy. And *this* is precisely the crucial point used by Wicksell as a lever for his own critique. His exposition, however, is not as straightforward as it appears from the above; but the ultimate conclusions are none the less the same. In fact, what Wicksell does not really accept in Ricardo is the vision of an always-convergent economic system towards its 'normal' position and that any deviations from this would only be accidental and ultimately would not influence that position in any respect. One aspect of this Ricardian conception consists in the missing explanation of the *process* through which one starts from a certain cause to get some effects.

Let us consider more closely this aspect of the Wicksellian critique and its implications. Wicksell writes:

> Ricardo never examined in detail by *what means* the banks could succeed in putting a larger amount of their stocks of money or notes into circulation and especially *what effects* the lowering of the loan rate would have on the demand for credit instruments and on the level of prices. (Wicksell, 1906, p. 178; italics added)

In this connection the Ricardian position is made explicit in the following passage in which it is maintained that the money rate of interest is not regulated by the rate at which the Bank will lend, whether it be 5, 4, or 3 per cent, but by the rate of profits which can be made by the employment of capital, and which is totally independent of the quantity, or of the value of money. Whether a Bank lent one million, ten millions, or a hundred millions, they would not permanently alter the market rate of interest; they would alter only the value of the money which they thus issued. (Ricardo, 1951a, pp. 363–4; italics added)[7]

The word 'permanently' is important, since it does exactly reflect Ricardo's basic idea according to which monetary phenomena cannot influence those pertaining to the system of production – save temporarily. This idea is much more clearly expressed in another place. It will be convenient to quote entirely the passage referred to now:

I do not dispute, that if the Bank were to bring a large additional sum of notes into the market, and offer them on loan, but that they would for a time affect the rate of interest. The same effects would follow from the discovery of a hidden treasure of gold or silver coin. If the amount were large, the Bank, or the owner of the treasure, might not be able to lend the notes or the money at four, nor perhaps, above three per cent; but having done so, neither the notes, nor the money, would be retained unemployed by the borrowers; they would be sent into every market, and would everywhere raise the prices of commodities, till they were absorbed in the general circulation. It is only *during the interval* of the issues of the Bank, and their effect on prices, that we should be sensible of an abundance of money; interest would, *during that interval*, be under its natural level; but as soon as the additional sum of notes or of money became absorbed in the general circulation, the rate of interest would be as high, and new loans would be demanded with as much eagerness as before the additional issues. (Ricardo, 1951b, p. 91; italics added)

Wicksell concedes to Ricardo the conclusions of his reasoning on strictly *logical* grounds, rejecting at the same time the content of his *analysis*. The pivot of the whole Ricardian argument is the existence of automatic market mechanisms, working at any time and at the right moment to reestablish equilibrium; although coherent from a logical point of view (the reference should be the equation of exchange), that kind of reasoning leads ultimately to a view in which monetary phenomena leave no trace on the long-run 'real' position.

Ricardo, in fact, in order to give further support to his thesis – according to which a permanent lowering of the rate of interest is excluded – makes use of a paradoxical case (Ricardo, 1951b, p. 92). He imagines what sort of consequences would follow if the banks issued money to be loaned at interest rates far below the 'normal' level: strong competition would take place among the industries of the system leading to abnormally low profits for which no other system could be as competitive as that considered – except in the case where a similar interest rate policy would have been adopted by the other economic system. That is absurd, according to Ricardo, since the system in which that interest rate reduction took place would be able to absorb the whole of world commerce. He thus confirms his theory on the non-contamination between monetary and productive phenomena: profits 'can only be lowered by a competition of capital not consisting of circulating medium' (ibid), which is the twin statement of another according to which 'the rate of interest for money is totally independent of the nominal amount of the circulating medium' (ibid, p. 143).

The Ricardo reasoning so far considered, directed at showing the impossibility of having a permanent reduction in the money rate of interest, seems to Wicksell self-contradictory, both with respect to his own theory of comparative costs[8] and with respect to other aspects of his thought on monetary questions. As regards the former aspect, in fact, Wicksell points out that if the reduction in the interest rate (necessary to put into circulation a greater quantity of money) should reduce production costs (and so prices), then the need for credit instruments would be diminishing instead of increasing, in such a way that no increase of the quantity of money in circulation would be possible. To avoid the latter possibility one has to imagine the opposite: namely, an increase in production costs (and so in prices). This would be in line with what Ricardo often maintains: an increase in the quantity of money leads to an export of the metal and to an import of commodities; hence a *decreased* capacity of commodity export, not an increased one – as he previously affirmed.

The pointing-out of this contradiction in Ricardo does not put an end to Wicksell's critique. The latter emphasised not so much the content of that contradiction, rather the wholly missing explanation of the process which would lead to the Ricardian thesis:

But Ricardo's argument by no means explains *why, how, and to what extent* a lower rate of interest has this effect, which is the essence of the whole problem. (Wicksell, 1906, p. 181; italics added)

This remark refers to the basic aspect of Wicksell's disagreement with Ricardo: in the analysis of the latter there is an empty space to fill. Wicksell does not subscribe to the fundamental role attributed by Ricardo to the automatic mechanism of adjustment; he emphasises instead the far more important role of the banking system and its economic power.[9] Parallel to this is the objection to Ricardo's identification of the monetary economy with the monetary system.[10] On the contrary, according to Wicksell the monetary economy should be defined jointly by the monetary *and* the productive systems, whereas for Ricardo it is the latter which is ultimately of exclusive importance. Wicksell does want to fill the 'empty space' referred to above by putting forward all the complexities through which the two systems can and should be joined: the aim of his research is essentially defined in this way. As regards this point it is convenient to point out by now that no unique way exists to solve that 'dichotomy'. However, the way pursued subsequently by the literature has completely avoided the issue, compressing the monetary system to the productive one, thus getting an unacceptable definition for a monetary economy.

The methodological problem raised by Wicksell against Ricardo is of much more importance than one would at first imagine, and the Ricardian legacy, as it emerges from his 'monetary' papers, did have a non-negligible weight in this connection.

NOTES

1. Here and henceforth references to Wicksell will show the original year of publication, whereas page numbers will refer to the corresponding English edition (if available). Page numbers of any other reference will correspond to the edition referred to by the year of publication.
2. We encounter here the 'pure credit' hypothesis first formulated by Wicksell in his scheme which will be considered in Chapter 2. It suffices, however, to point out that according to the above hypothesis commercial exchange takes place simply by means of bookkeeping at the banks; the latter – once the loan rate of interest is fixed – concede any amount of loan demanded by the entrepreneurs.

3. It should be noted that the above example can also be adopted to the case of an improvement in transport conditions of commodities.
4. See also T. Haavelmo (1978) on Wicksell's attitude in this respect.
5. A different approach in the analysis of Wicksell's critique of Ricardo is given by S. Di Gaspare (1979, part. I, chs 4, 5, 6).
6. The canonical example is offered by Patinkin's work (1965), which will be considered in detail in Chapter 5. It should be remembered that monetary problems have always been present in Ricardo's elaboration both before and after his *Principles*, and that his ideas on those problems did not undergo any relevant change (see R. S. Sayers, 1953, sec. VI).
7. Ricardo's idea, explicity considered elsewhere (1951b, pp. 88–9) according to which the rate of interest is ultimately determined by non-monetary factors, is present here. Wicksell will always object to this idea (encountered even in other writers after Ricardo) which identifies interest with the remuneration for the use of (real) capital and not of money (cf. Wicksell, 1898b, p. 245).
8. Wicksell points out that the circumstances adduced by Ricardo are plainly in contrast to what the latter maintained in his theory of foreign trade (Ricardo, 1951a, ch. 7; and Wicksell, 1906, p. 180). One country can be absolutely superior in the production of all commodities and nonetheless have benefits in trading with other countries. Ricardo's argument, in effect, leaves aside too many elements and gives too-scanty information (e.g. on technology, wage-levels) to be fully accepted.
9. From a different viewpoint, R. S. Sayers (1953, pp. 93–4) points out that the Ricardian emphasis on the long-term forces 'prevented him from realizing the potentialities of banking policy, but also lent to much of his exposition an air of unreality that weakened its political effect'.

    This methodological attitude of Ricardo can be found also in his theory of foreign trade (see M. De Cecco, 1974, ch. 1).

    An opposing opinion is maintained by A. W. Marget (1966, p. 98) according to which the Wicksellian doctrine 'with respect to the relation between money and the rate of interest was identical with the heart of Ricardian doctrine on the subject'. Along the same lines, see J. Åkerman (1933, pp. 116–17).
10. At the *analytical* level, one should notice, it is not necessary for 'money' to be explicitly present, in order to frame a 'monetary economy'. For example, the system of production in Sraffa's scheme is only *one side* of the economy considered, and in contrast to Ricardo it does not coincide with the whole. In this connection it suffices to recall Sraffa's case when workers share in the surplus: under this circumstance the rate of profits is 'susceptible of being determined from outside the system of production, in particular by the level of the money rates of interest' (Sraffa, 1960, p. 33).

2 The Theoretical Scheme

2.1

The aim of this chapter is to provide a schematic reference-framework of Wicksell's monetary theory. The 'reference' feature should be constantly remembered. In fact, the task of the present work is limited to pointing out and discussing some critical points in Wicksell's monetary theory whose further development could furnish new elements for a critique of the traditional monetary theory. Within the boundaries so defined no systematic alternative theory will be formulated – this task could perhaps be pursued at a subsequent stage.

In Chapters 3 and 4 a detailed process of Wicksell's elaboration will be illustrated (regarding his scheme of a monetary economy); they must then be considered as a digression with respect to the theoretical scheme of this chapter.

For that scheme, whose characteristics will presently be shown, the direct references are to *Interest and Prices* and to *Lectures on Political Economy*, vol. II (here and henceforth *Lectures II*).

2.2

What the Wicksellian theory, now under discussion, aims to consistently bring forth are the conditions under which variations in the general price level take place.

Among those conditions a decisive role pertains to the banking system in acting as an 'intermediary' between those who want to save (thus supplying funds for investment) and those who want to invest (thus demanding funds to undertake their production plans) – although, as will be seen subsequently, the character of that 'intermediation' is completely different from the traditional one.

It is obviously necessary to make certain hypotheses in order to define unambiguously the scheme in which the problem referred to above is rigorously analysed.

As a first approximation an economy whose 'production system' is assumed to be constant over time is taken into account. Specifically, the assumption is of an economic system in a 'stationary state', i.e. a system in which the 'services' rendered by workers and landowners are utilised by the entrepreneurs in the productive processes in order to furnish exclusively a given quantity of consumers' goods for society as a whole, as well as to *repair* those goods 'which contribute to output, either with or without the assistance of further labour and land' and 'which have a very high and sometimes unlimited *durability*. Examples are provided by houses, streets, railways, canals, certain improvements in land, certain kinds of machines' – goods defined by Wicksell as 'rent-earnings goods' (Wicksell, 1898b, p. 126).

In these circumstances it is then logical to assume – as Wicksell does – constant relative market prices and therefore equality between quantities demanded and supplied. Under such a hypothesis capital accumulation is completely ruled out; only variations in magnitudes expressed in *monetary* terms can take place – whose conditions will be examined subsequently. The distinction between capital accumulation, in terms referred to above, and variations in monetary income is based on the corresponding distinction, unambiguous in Wicksell, between 'real' and 'monetary' capital.

'Real' capital accumulation materialises itself in the production of production goods – goods, that is to say, needed to increase the quantity of consumption goods in the *future*. For this purpose, however, it is necessary to undertake an act of *saving* in the *present*, an act, in other words, which enables *from the beginning* the setting-up of those processes directed to produce production goods. In concrete terms, an act of saving allows productive resources (labour and land) to be employed in the production of production goods instead of consumption goods.

An example given by Wicksell will make more clear what has been said so far:

> A landowner who saves a part of his income subscribes and pays for shares or bonds in a neighbouring railway which is under construction. With the money so obtained, the railway board pays a number of workmen, who provide themselves with milk and other foodstuffs from the landowner's land. The landowner, in proportion as the money flows back to him, re-invests it in shares or bonds; and so on. The landowner might, if he so wished, directly consume the product of this labour, if, for example, he employed the same workmen as beaters in a hunt. Instead, the labour is now used in a saved-up form in order to render future railway traffic

possible. This is the *accumulation of real capital*. If we add to our illustration horses, which in the one case may be used for hunting and in the other may be hired out by the landowner for a cash payment as beasts of burden for building the railway, we shall thereby include another element in capital, *saved up natural resources*, in so far as we regard the value of pasturage, hay, oats, etc., used for the feeding of such horses, as essentially representing the rent of land. Even the most complex forms of capital accumulation and transfer, as well as the transformation of existing capital, may be analysed in the same way. Here, too, as we have seen, money transactions only represent the *form* of real economic phenomena; any quantity of money, however small, would evidently be adequate to effect any amount of capital accumulation or capital transfer whatever. In other words, the quantity of money and the quantity of capital in a country bear no necessary relation to each other whatever. (Wicksell, 1906, p. 25)

Together with the hypothesis of a stationary state there is also the supposition that each process has the same duration, starting and ending at the same moment of time: at the beginning of the period labour and natural resources are simultaneously 'applied', according to the techniques in use; at the end of the production period only consumption goods come out as products.

The entrepreneurs constitute a class of individuals who supervise the productive processes, decide and make operative the investment plans of the system. They manage *exclusively* with capital borrowed from the banking system for a period equal to that of production, having at their disposal only 'rent-earning goods' mentioned above. The possibility of self-financing productive investment as well as the possibility of establishing loan-contracts with non-banking institutions is ruled out. The possibility that individuals other than entrepreneurs undertake productive investment is also excluded. On the contrary, consumption is completely self-financed, ruling out in this way any loan which is not made for productive purpose.

The capitalists are treated on the same footing as 'pure rentiers'; they are also the merchants of all the commodities produced in the system, i.e. consumption goods, in a way which will be explained presently.

In order to illustrate how the transactions take place and to put forward at the same time the phenomena characterising the scheme

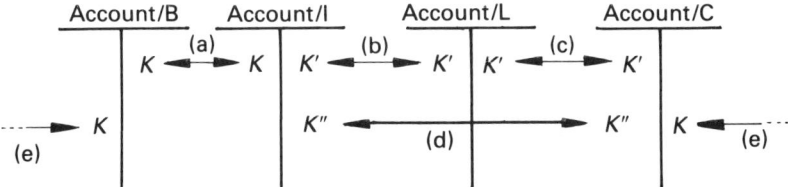

Figure 2.1

now under discussion, we can refer to an 'accounting system' for the economy as a whole.

For this let us imagine each class of individuals, banking system included, entitled with an account of 'credit–debit' type. The double arrows in Figure 2.1 and the letter written near each of them show the credit–debit movements which *logically* take place in the different phases of the process.

The sequence of operations will be as follows. At the *beginning* of the period considered the entrepreneurs (account/I) ask for a loan at the banks (account/B) whose amount is assumed to be K at the rate of interest of i, due at the end of the production period. The banks grant that loan: phase (a).

That amount is immediately divided into two parts: one K' goes as advanced payment to labourers and land-owners (here grouped together into a single account/L) as a remuneration for their services to be provided in the coming production: phase (b); the residual part (K'') goes to the entrepreneurs themselves as a remuneration for their managerial work. In this way we must have $K \equiv K' + K''$.

With the amount K' both labourers and land-owners will buy the necessary consumption goods from the capitalists (account/C) for the whole period considered: phase (c). The entrepreneurs will do the same with the amount K'': phase (d).

The capitalists, who are also the merchants, possess the entire 'consumption fund' of society (which is made up by the goods corresponding to K' and K'' together) plus a quantity of goods they hold for themselves – obviously not written in their account because it does not occasion any movement – which can be supposed to be equal to iK.

At the beginning of the period – which is the moment at which the operations are supposed to take place – the whole amount of consumption goods will be equal to $(1+i)K$.

The amount received by the capitalists from the workers, the land-owners and the entrepreneurs in payment for consumption goods is paid into the banks' account (account/B): phase (*e*).

Always at the beginning of each period this is the amount which is lent to the entrepreneurs, and so the cycle begins and goes on in the same way.

As can be easily verified all the accounts balance.

It is worth noting that the banks could lend the requested amount in any form whatsoever. If metallic money is used, and the loan given to only one group of entrepreneurs, the phases of the cycle will follow till that amount of metallic money again returns to the banks; now the banks are able to make a new loan to another group of entrepreneurs, and so on, till the point is reached where all of them result in being receivers of the loan. In such circumstances the metallic money would circulate as many times as is necessary to end all the operations.

At the opposite extreme lies the case in which no money circulates at all and in which the operations take place by means of cheques drawn on the banks (pure credit); in this case loan operations would take place once and for all.

The hypothesis of sharply distinguishing the role of the entrepreneurs from that of the capitalists implies that the whole amount of loan given by the banks is equal to the value of consumption goods necessary to get the production processes started.

It follows quite obviously that in so far as some capitalists are also entrepreneurs the necessary amount of the loan required for the productive cycle is correspondingly reduced, and the reasoning will be made in terms of a certain *proportion* of the loan with respect to the value of consumption goods – which is of course always possible to make without influencing the results.

The rate of interest on loan (i) is assumed to be equal to the deposit rate.[1] Here too a different hypothesis would be without any consequence on the logical structure of the scheme.

Let us now turn to the phasing of the transactions *at the end* of the period in terms of the accounting (Figure 2.2).

The capitalists credit an amount of interest to iK on their own deposit K at the banks: phase (*a*).

The entrepreneurs sell to the capitalists – phase (b) – an amount of commodities produced, *as much as is necessary* to extinguish their debt made previously with the banks and due exactly at the end of the period of production: phase (*c*).

The Theoretical Scheme

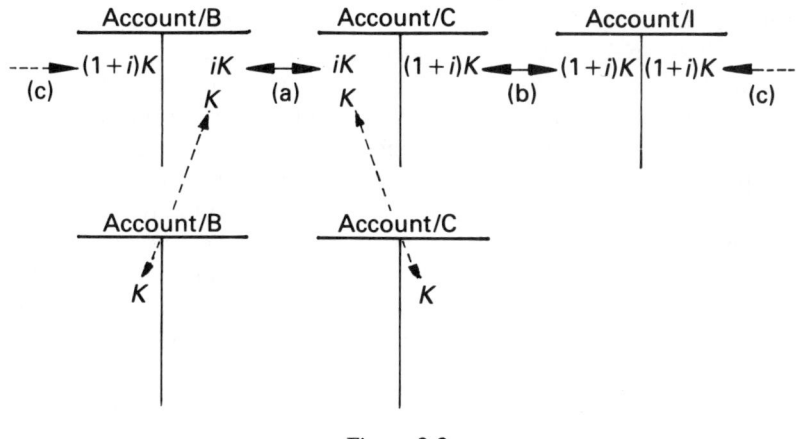

Figure 2.2

Even now all the accounts balance.

At the moment in which the operations are examined it is shown that the capitalists possess an amount of consumption goods equal to $(1+i)K$. Of this, they will hold a part equal to iK for their own consumption and the other, equal to K, will be at their disposal for the production of the subsequent period (the broken arrows in Figure 2.2 show the corresponding amount in the accounts of the banks and of the capitalists at the *beginning* of the subsequent period). The cycle is then in the process of repeating itself in the same way as illustrated above.

At this point however it is necessary to make some considerations before going on.

2.3

A fundamental hypothesis of the process so far described was expressed by the *unchanged* conditions pertaining to the reference scheme. The latter, in particular, is characterised by an 'equilibrium' having: (i) the general price level constant (monetary equilibrium); (ii) equality between quantities demanded and supplied (productive equilibrium).[2]

This particular state of the economic system, however, is simply taken into consideration by Wicksell as a 'means' for analysing a non-equilibrium situation (as the most probable) and the relation between the two: *this* is in fact the central topic on which the whole Wicksellian analysis is focused, as will be shown later on.

For this purpose it is then necessary to imagine that one of the above equilibrium conditions is not realised, i.e. either on the side of the banking system or on the productive one. From a strictly analytical point of view either of them leads to the same result, but on economic ground Wicksell rightly regards the productive system as the most pertinent place from which a 'break' in the equilibrium position originates instead of the credit policy put forward by the banking system. One can thus ask why the banks should, for example, lower the rate of interest 'other things being equal' (Wicksell, 1898a, p. 81).

The clue to the reasoning lies in regarding more realistically the 'primum movens', as Wicksell says, springing from the conditions of production and distribution, which before were regarded as unchanged, whereas in the meantime an *unchanged* banking policy of money interest rate is supposed. It is, however, necessary to express the 'conditions of production and distribution' in a way in which a comparison can be made between these on the one hand and the 'conditions of money market' concisely expressed by the money rate of interest on the other. The money rate of interest, Wicksell writes:

> can never be either high or low *in itself*, but only in relation to the return which can, or is expected to, be obtained by the man who is in possession of money. (Wicksell, 1897, p. 236)[3]

The content of this statement is identically reproduced in other places (cf. Wicksell, 1898a, p. 80, and 1898b, pp. xxiv–xxv). The magnitude which expresses that effective or potential gain is called by Wicksell 'normal', 'real' or 'natural' rate of interest:

> What I called the normal rate of interest is anything but a fixed magnitude valid at any time, it is changeable over time. It basically means a commercial interest, a real interest on the capitals employed in the various firms . . ., that is that interest one could call the natural interest on capital; a concept whose exact formulation is practically and theoretically one of the most difficult tasks. (Wicksell, 1897, p. 236)[4]

This latter phrase contains *all* the difficulties which Wicksell points out on every occasion when that concept has to be introduced –

difficulties, however, which belong to the very conditions on which it is built rather than to the concept itself. To this we will return again later. For the time being it is convenient to formulate the hypothesis of a change in the conditions of production and distribution as the factor from which a *difference* between the two rates so far considered originates, i.e. the *money* and the *natural* rates of interest. One can suppose, for example, technical progress taking place in one or more industries of the system; or some variation in the distribution of income. These cases will correspondingly give rise to a variation in the profitability of production such as to alter the supposed equality between the money and the natural rates of interest. (In this connection see Wicksell's case of an increase in real wages – Wicksell, 1898a, pp. 81–2.)

As opposed to the variations in the interest rate that are due to the banking policy, those produced in the production and distribution field take place continuously; thus a variation of the natural rate 'belongs to everyday phenomena' (Wicksell, 1897, p. 239).

> In the customary behaviour of the banks one can always find a bias not to increase or decrease without *urgent* need the interest rates. In the circumstance in which neither a single bank nor in the long run all the banks of a single country *are* even partially able to change their interest rates, there plainly lies a strong reason for the maintenance of the general interest rates; whereas the natural rate on capital is subject to all the thousand and one circumstances which define the modern commercial life, and its average level increases or decreases continuously. (Wicksell, 1897, p. 239)

Thus:

> following an increased demand for loans, the banks decide to raise their interest rates, the natural interest can in the meantime continue its increase, or it can take place in the case referred to above [inflationary expectations], in which the market has already begun to take into account *increasing* prices and, as a consequence, a *moderate* increase in the interest is not able any more to curb the increasing movement of prices. In other words, during these periods, a more or less constant difference will take place between the natural interest on capital, which is increasing, and the money interest, which is increasing too but more sluggishly, and this in the way previously said must continuously push prices upward. (Wicksell, 1897, pp. 239)

Under these circumstances a very important dynamic element is then introduced into the scheme, this being the *non-instantaneous* adaptation of the bank rate policy to the changed economic conditions. If it is true that *after* a more or less long period of time an adaptation of the money rate to the natural rate of interest is conceivable, nonetheless the nature of the process that *in the meantime* is taking place remains an open question.

Thus, the statement according to which under the hypothesis of a money rate of interest relatively lower than the natural one an increased demand for loans induces a corresponding increase in the money rate, such as to fill up the difference between the two rates, belongs to a *successive* stage in the analysis, whose contents have to be studied separately from those pertaining to the 'first instance' analysis.

2.4

The entire chapter 8 of Wicksell's *Interest and Prices* is devoted to the natural rate of interest and to the relationship between this and the money rate. This chapter appears as a preliminary to what Wicksell calls the 'systematic exposition of the theory'. Before dealing with the latter it seems convenient to concentrate on some crucial points of the chapter mentioned above.

Wicksell's efforts in this chapter are directed towards giving substance to the concept 'natural rate of interest'. For this purpose he takes as a starting reference point a barter economy, in which four classes of individuals are supposed to exist, defined on the basis of their respective *functions* with regard the economic process: labourers, land-owners, entrepreneurs and capitalists.

The entrepreneurs, who are the managers of the productive processes, operate exclusively with 'capital' loaned from the capitalists – and with the supposition that the transactions are made *in natura*; the capitalists are the 'lenders' of the system as well as the 'merchants' of the goods.

In order to give concreteness to a 'natural rate of interest' for the economy as a whole two alternative hypotheses can be admitted. In the first, it is supposed that for each commodity an equilibrium between demand and supply prevails; in the second, such an equilibrium is supposed not to take place. The first of these two hypotheses, as we shall presently see, corresponds to the simplified version of a stationary state envisaged by Wicksell in his scheme, whereas the second hypothesis, more general and in any case adaptable to the Wicksellian scheme, regards an economic system in a 'moving' position, outside the stationary state. It will be useful, to make the analysis complete, to say something on this second case – even though the scheme so far considered was exclusively confined to an economy in a stationary state.[5]

In the supposed second case, that regarding the divergence between demand and supply (no matter how many commodities), some price movements must necessarily take place. To illustrate this, let us take as an example an economic system in which only two commodities, a and b, are produced. Let us suppose that, starting from an equilibrium between demand and supply, an alteration in the quantities demanded takes place such that for commodity a demand is greater than supply, and therefore for commodity b the opposite is true.[6]

In this new situation the price of commodity a will go up, whereas the price of commodity b will go down. These price-movements, in the directions indicated now, would then constitute the basis for an *expectation* of an *increase* in the future supply of commodity a (or, what turns to be the same thing, an *expectation* of a *lower* price in the future – that is at the moment in which the new equilibrium is supposed to be established – relative to the present price); for the same reason an *expectation* in the opposite direction for commodity b will be generated.

If one now takes as a reference commodity a and supposes a loan is made just for the period in which those price-movements take place, the *natural* rate of interest for commodity a (measured in terms of and with respect to itself) will be *higher* than the correspondent *natural* rate of interest for commodity b, measured for the same period and in an identical way. This is so, in the first case considered, because one has to *add* the difference between the present price and the price supposed to prevail in the future (per unit of commodity) to the established interest (per unit of commodity); the necessity of undertaking this procedure is based on the obvious fact that at the end of the period considered one unit of commodity a will command a *lower* quantity of commodity b. (Following the same line of reasoning, the natural rate of interest for commodity b will be lower than the corresponding rate for commodity a.)

The divergence of these 'natural' rates is just another aspect of the same phenomenon on which the above discussion was based, i.e. a divergence between demand and supply of commodities.[7] Given the characteristics of a competitive market, here supposed, that divergence will be influential on the *transition* from one equilibrium to another (in terms of demand and supply).

The discussion so far substantially reproduces the own-rates of interest theory formulated by Sraffa in his already quoted review of von Hayek's book (Hayek, 1931; Sraffa, 1932). As is well known, it was put forward again by Keynes (1936, p. 223); however, both he and others, who subsequently rescued that theory (cf. Lerner, 1952, pp. 173–80; Conard, 1959, pp. 199–30),[8] skipped the *context* in which it was first formulated.

And that context was actually a series of arguments postulated by Hayek *against* Wicksell.

Thus Sraffa, in criticising Hayek provides at the same time a coherent reference-framework in which it seems possible to include some of Wicksell's arguments, probably made by the latter in an intuitive and rougher way. In fact, it is not an accident that in Sraffa's exposition one can also find an echo of many propositions contained in the already quoted chapter 8 of *Interest and Prices* (Sraffa, 1932).[9]

At this point it is necessary to reconsider the natural rate of interest contained in the Wicksellian scheme.

In the light of what has been so far illustrated it seems possible to formulate two alternative notions of that rate, according to whether an economy is taken in equilibrium, in terms of demand and supply, or not. As we have seen, in the first case a *unique* natural rate of interest comes into being in a straightforward way. In the second case, however, there exist as many rates as there are commodities – although one can obviously envisage *one* average of them.[10]

Wicksell, as said above, makes use of the simplest case for his scheme – namely, that in which equality between demand and supply prevails, for which case constant relative market prices can be supposed. This might be explained by considering that the basic aim of his research was to define phenomena for which the assumption of a given economic system and a given natural rate of interest was sufficient. Nonetheless he seems to perceive, even if only to a very slight extent, the complexities of the latter case considered.

First of all, he emphasised on various occasions – as elsewhere noted – that the level of the natural rate of interest 'is not fixed or unalterable in magnitude' (1898b, p. 106). Moreover, 'it depends on all the thousand and one things which determine the current economic position of a community: and with them it constantly fluctuates'

The Theoretical Scheme

(ibid). From this, and having in mind the stickiness in the movement of the money rates of interest, one can deduce that

> *exact* coincidence of the two rates of interest is therefore unlikely. For changes in the (average) natural rate may be presumed (on the basis of the Law of Large Numbers) to be continuous, while the money rate of interest is usually raised or lowered only in discontinuous jumps of one-half or one per cent, at any rate in so far as it is regulated by the large monetary institutions. (Wicksell, 1898b, p. 106)

Following as an immediate corollary of such a position is the proposition that the levelling-out of the two rates should always be considered a *tendency* (ibid, p. 117):

> In the interest of accuracy, we have purposely avoided the statement that for the maintenance of stable prices it is necessary that the money and natural rates should be *equal*. In practice they are both rather vague conceptions, if it is a general mean level that is under discussion, and their exact determination, even from the theoretical point of view, involves great difficulties. (ibid, p. 120)[11]

Here, the 'relative' concept of the level of the money rate of interest comes in again. Actually by comparing *directly* this magnitude with the general level of prices it is not surprising *not* to find any symmetry between movements of the former and movements of the latter: a given movement in money prices, for instance increasing, could alternately be associated with a lower, or a higher, or unchanged money rate. The reason for this, as in a different way observed above, lies in the corresponding movement of the *natural* rate, which the former must ultimately be compared with.

This remark points out another phenomenon, regarding the impossibility of actually ascertaining the natural rate of interest, in order to establish a certain levelling-out between those two rates. However, since there are three magnitudes under consideration – somehow correlated one to each other – that rate ultimately becomes a case of secondary importance: 'the connecting link', as Wicksell expressed it (1898b, p. 109), between those two rates is just the general price level; then, for example, as the latter increases (or decreases more and more slowly) it is possible to maintain that the relationship between the money rate and the natural rate is such that the former turns out to be lower than the latter. It goes without saying, that the importance of this fact greatly simplifies decisions about which bank rate policy to adopt.

2.5

Let us consider now the case of a change in the conditions of production such that, for example, they induce an increased demand for funds in order to finance the productive activity – this is so, one can imagine, because the entrepreneurs come to believe, from a point of time on, upon a 'natural' rate *relatively superior* to that which ruled before. Also in this case it makes no difference which cause determines the relative increase of the 'natural' rate; what matters is the possibility of making such a hypothesis.

We can perhaps see more clearly how that can happen if we turn our attention to considering the value of the consumption goods retained by the entrepreneurs as a remuneration for themselves, relative to the period considered. (That magnitude was early represented by K''.)

During the description of the development of the book-keeping operations it was put forward that at the end of the period the entrepreneurs sell to the merchant-capitalists an amount of the whole production as much as is *necessary* to extinguish the debts which the former contracted with the banks. Therefore they do *not* necessarily sell the *whole* production they possess. The amount they sell to the capitalists is equal, as already seen, to $(1+i)K$, since they are obliged to extinguish a debt of the amount K contracted at the beginning of the period at the rate of interest equal to i, and thus they must be able to cash a sum of money equal to *that* amount. However, the value of their production, at current prices, can obviously be *different* from that at which they sell to the capitalists. Let us suppose the value of the production at the end of the period – production consisting, as already said, exclusively of consumption goods – be equal to C; therefore with a money capital employed equal to K one gets the equation $(1+i')K = C$, in which i' can be considered the 'natural' rate of interest. (Note that the relative market prices are given and constant throughout the period considered.)

The value of the consumption goods the entrepreneurs assign to themselves *as a whole* as a remuneration for their managerial work can then be distinguished into two parts: one equal to K'', which is the 'normal' remuneration: another which consists of the difference between the value of the *whole* production, equal to $(1+i')K=C$, and the value of the production *sold* to the capitalists, equal to $(1+i)K$. This difference, equal to $(i'-i)K$, can be considered as a 'surplus' remuneration, being positive or negative as $i'>i$ or $i'<i$.

Let us suppose the natural rate of interest to be greater than the loan rate of interest ($i'>i$). In such a case there *exists* a positive 'surplus' remuneration. What are the effects on the economic system of such a 'surplus'?

The entrepreneurs can choose two ways in order to realise their 'surplus' remuneration:

(1) exchanging among themselves the corresponding quantity of goods and laying them on one side for the consumption of the coming year; while they offer the rest of their stocks to the capitalists (Wicksell, 1898b, p. 142);
(2) by offering it entirely to the capitalists (ibid).

In the latter case, by simply offering a greater quantity of goods a variation in the distribution between demand and supply does not necessarily follow. In fact, by selling to the capitalists the *whole* production obtained at a value equal to $(1+i')K$ the entrepreneurs would realise a 'surplus' in monetary terms equal to $(i'-i)K$ in any case, thus in the following period they can *increase* their demand in proportion to that amount, and consequently no divergence would arise between demand and supply.

Therefore, the pure *existence* of a 'surplus' devoted, as already pointed out, either to the *consumption* or to the *market* does not imply any variation in the general level of prices. It is like supposing that the difference $(i'-i)$ does not exist because that 'surplus' *in itself* is unable to produce some mechanism leading to variations in the distribution between demand and supply.

One can obviously illustrate this latter point in terms of the book-keeping system used in the previous pages.

If the entrepreneurs, as already said, sell to the capitalists the whole production of the period, this is reflected in the book-keeping system in the fact that in the accounts, of which the latter is formed, a different amount (K^*) is substituted for the amount K – keeping K', C and i as they stand – which is greater than before and determined in the following way:

$$C = (1 + i') K = (1 + i) K^*;$$

whereas K'' is replaced by $K''+(K^*-K)$. In other words this difference has been simply 'incorporated' into the book-keeping system; *as such* it disappeared, thus the new system will replicate the same dynamics as before, with the only variation, of course, that now the *new* magnitudes referred to above will appear.

One moment of reflection can reveal *why* the 'surplus' remuneration is unable in itself to put in motion any mechanism different from those appearing period after period in a system such as that so far considered.

First of all, the entrepreneurs must be able to *realise* that the 'surplus' effectively represents a remuneration above that considered as 'normal', above that remuneration 'for the trouble of conducting his business as he would have obtained for conducting a similar business on behalf of others' (Wicksell, 1898b, p. 140).

Being fully aware of this, then *production* will be involved – in the way presently illustrated – not simply the *consumption* or the *market*, as previously considered.

> If entrepreneurs continue, year after year perhaps, to realise some surplus profit of this kind, the result can only be to set up a tendency for an expansion of their activities. (Wicksell, 1898b, p. 143)

In such a case, therefore, the fact that the natural rate of interest is greater than the money rate will no longer be *latent* in the system, and it will become *effective*; this, from another point of view can be regarded on the same footing as a *credit facility*, measured by the difference between the natural rate and the money rate of interest.

The entrepreneurs, then, will seek to corner the productive services in order to expand their production. However, if the resources are already fully occupied, this will necessarily produce only a *tendency* for the expansion and not an effective one.

2.6

The hypothesis of full employment of the resources, within the Wicksellian framework, should be interpreted in a different way from a simple working hypothesis. What in effect one wants to essentially point out in the present framework is the different degree of elasticity (or response) to some economic variable with respect to others, relative to the entrepreneurs' willingness to accumulate.

In any *given moment*, in fact, if on the basis of a 'surplus' obtained the entrepreneurs want to expand their production, it is quite probable they will be halted by the constraint of the 'natural' resources, which are *limited*, compared with the supply of funds made available by the banks for the accumulation, which are *unlimited*.

The inflationary process, whose features will be illustrated presently, is just a reflection of the fact already mentioned. A general expansion of production cannot be made at will, nor can one say beforehand how long it takes to make it economically possible:

> It is impossible to endorse the widespread view that under suitable conditions a country's output can be expanded almost indefinitely, by 'arousing the spirit of enterprise' and the like. This fallacious view is derived by concentrating attention on one single branch of production, provided perhaps with an excess of fixed capital (buildings, machines, etc.). In such a single branch of production it would be possible to increase output immediately, but only at *the expense of the other branches of production* from which labour and liquid capital have to be drawn. . . . A *general* expansion of production would thus be possible only as a result of longer hours – which are neither desirable nor feasible over any length of time – or as a result of further technical progress. (Wicksell, 1898b, p. 143)

Let us check what happens once the tendency to that expansion is admitted.

In the first place the entrepreneurs ask the banks, at the beginning of the production period, for an amount of loans necessary to finance a productive activity potentially larger than before (since the natural rate is now supposed to be higher) with the same prices of the previous period – the prices are retained constant by the entrepreneurs also for the following period. The financial requirement can then be entirely satisfied:

> We have seen that in our ideal state every payment, and consequently every loan, is accomplished by means of cheques or *giro* facilities. No matter what amount of money may be demanded from the banks, that is the amount which they are in a position to lend. (Wicksell, 1898b, p. 110)

After that 'the business of lending money and of exchanging commodities remains at a standstill throughout the rest of the year, production sets in at the beginning of the year and continues without interruption until end' (Wicksell, 1898b, p. 140).

The entrepreneurs, with the proceeds of the sales from the last period *plus* the new funds just borrowed, will compete in buying resources, giving rise in this way to an increased demand for labour and other productive forces. The incomes (money wages and rents) will increase correspondingly:

> It is impossible to tell directly how much wages will go up, and therefore by how much industrial capital has to be increased. But on our assumption it is possible to fix a limit. If entrepreneurs are not reckoning for the moment on any rise in future prices, the upper limit to the possible rise in wages is the fall in the rate of interest. For the sake of simplicity, it will be supposed that this upper limit is immediately attained. (Wicksell, 1898b, p. 144)

On the other hand, the increase in revenues – even if exactly equal to the admitted credit facility – does not make the 'surplus' remuneration disappear. At the end of the period, in fact, when the consumption goods are ready for the market there will be an increased demand for them (due to the increase in the revenues); but at the same time there will also be a quantity of unchanged supply and this will necessarily produce an increase in the commodity prices (ibid, p. 144).

By supposing a perfectly uniform change of the latter throughout all sectors of the economy, the money capital (K), the fund of wages and rents (K') and the 'normal' remuneration (K'') will all increase in the *same proportion*.

This will mean that from a formal point of view the *same* bookkeeping system as before will remain equally suitable to describe the new situation characterised by an inflationary process, but at the same time by a productive structure identically equal to the previous one in every other respect.

The system can constantly repeat itself, except that, period after period, the inflationary process will reproduce itself too, becoming in this way *cumulative*.

This process could theoretically reach a stop *if* the banks increased the money rate at the same level as the natural rate. But the only effect would be to halt the present inflationary process – *ceteris paribus* – not to reestablish the general price level from which it started (ibid, p. 147).

As a matter of fact, the difference between the natural and the money rate is exclusively responsible for *variations* in the price level and not for its absolute height also.

2.7

Wicksell himself realised the necessity of introducing some modifications in his scheme, but they, as we shall see in a moment, do not undermine the basic reasoning contained in it.

In this fashion, the hypothesis made at the beginning according to which all the production processes start and end at the same moment can be relaxed without loss of generality. What would happen in this case would simply be a development of the processes at irregular time intervals with a consequent overlapping of them, which will produce a more rapid increase of the general price level.

As soon as prices start to increase, this will immediately lay the basis for the economic calculation of the new commercial contracts and agreements on remuneration (Wicksell, 1898b, p. 146). With the same period of time the cumulative process will be much more rapid:

> It has to be remembered that actual processes of exchange and payment do not take place at these annual intervals but follow on one another in rapid succession, so that one transaction is constantly 'infecting' another, to use Marx's phrase.[12] Furthermore, one particular lot of goods is in the normal run of business speculatively bought and sold many times over if the prospect of profits provides a sufficient inducement. There is thus no doubt that tremendous fluctuations in price may be brought about by some cause which is quite trivial in itself although it has real and lasting effects. (Wicksell, 1898b, p. 148)

The 'continuity' of such a process will surely be the most pertinent field in which the entrepreneurs will make up their *expectations* for increasing prices (ibid, p. 148). The same thing would happen even under the simple hypothesis of cycles occurring at 'regular intervals'. However, such expectations must necessarily be formed *with reference* to concrete data emerging from experience. Of this Wicksell seems fully aware by admitting, *not* as a simplifying hypothesis but as a first step of the development, just the opposite, namely that entrepreneurs make their own calculations in the first instance with reference to constant prices.

The persistence of the cumulative process – and the existence of a 'surplus' remuneration for the entrepreneurs – can also lead to another modification which would consist of a 'change of class': some capitalists would prefer to become entrepreneurs. In order for this phenomenon to take place, it is sufficient to suppose the banks allow the deposits at a lower rate of interest than they get from loans (Wicksell, 1898b, pp. 118, 148).

Under such circumstances the production turns out to be self-financed.

In any case, in order that a change of class takes place a certain amount of time would be necessary to allow the capitalist class to make that choice, which of course does not appear to be of a 'short run' character.

2.8

The transition from *Interest and Prices* to *Lectures II* does not seem to be an abandoning of Wicksell's monetary theory, nor a substantial revision of his main propositions as they were originally expressed. The basic theoretical scheme remains on the whole the same; what is going to be changed is the different viewpoint of *Lectures II* with respect to *Interest and Prices*.

In *Lectures II* one no longer finds a comparison between a monetary and a barter economy, but instead an analysis in which an economy where credit relationships are regulated directly between entrepreneurs and savers, is contrasted with one where these relationships take place through the banking system.

No apparent justification is offered for this change of viewpoint, and this suggests that Wicksell has become uncertain about the instrumental value of the distinction between a monetary and a non-monetary economy contained in *Interest and Prices*.

The different goal which characterises *Lectures II* compared with *Interest and Prices*, as well as the different public to whom the two works were respectively addressed, make it necessary that the exposition of the monetary theory contained in the first work be 'condensed' in one single section. This section appears, in *Lectures II*, as the 'positive solution' – as opposed to the other 'solutions' he has criticised in the chapter immediately before.

If this 'forced' synthesis makes it necessary for the reader to refer to some sections of *Interest and Prices*, it has nonetheless the advantage of putting forward the essential features of his basic monetary scheme.

The comparison made between an economy *without* and an economy *with* a banking system is addressed to point out, respectively, the different mechanisms operating in the system on the coordination between decisions to invest and to save. In the first case, such a coordination takes place through the *market* and the usual 'rules' regulating its functioning. Then the hypothesis of competition will make the connection between the natural and the money rates simple and direct. Any position outside the equilibrium will be immediately adjusted since the market itself, by definition, by allowing direct contacts between borrowers and lenders, establishes at the same time the 'price' at which no excess demand or supply exists.

There already exist on the market the mechanisms for making the correction. By assuming the existence of an equilibrium position – characterised by a rate of interest 'at which *the demand for loan capital and the supply of savings* exactly agree' (Wicksell, 1906, p. 193) – it will also be the *prevalent* position. On the market, in fact, non-equilibrium magnitudes do not stay for long in such a state: the non-equilibrium produces *ipso facto* the correction; the rate of interest existing *on the market* will be sensitive and will move in accordance with a demand different from supply.

In these circumstances, the 'historical' and the 'logical' time turn out to be almost identical; in other words, the monetary rate and the natural rate – although logically different from each other – are in this case practically the same (in the sense that a possible divergence between them cannot be but shortlived and transitory). What matters here is the *market* rate of interest, since on the market and through the market the two rates of interest can equalise themselves; or in other words decisions to invest and to save find an 'agreement'.

This still remains an abstract position; for more concretely, as Wicksell points out:

> A complete correspondence is of course not to be expected, if only for the reason that profit on capital is far from being a uniform conception, but varies greatly in different undertakings according as they are more or less successful. (Wicksell, 1906, p. 191)

The point to be stressed here is that in the case of credit taking place between man and man, which is now under discussion, the correction-mechanism is contained *inside* the theoretical scheme, and that this function is attributed *to the market*:

> If the prospects of the employment of capital become more promising, demand will increase and will at first exceed supply; interest rates will then rise and stimulate further saving at the same time as the demand from entrepreneurs contracts until a new equilibrium is reached at a slightly higher rate of interest. (Wicksell, 1906, p. 193)

Thus in the case of 'credit between man and man' no cumulative process takes place and so a credit expansion, for example, is *completely and exclusively* financed by private saving. An economy where credit takes place only between man and man is of course a 'primitive' economy compared with that in which the banking system does regularly enter into the reference scheme. However, the economic properties one can deduce from it can be auxiliary to those one wants to point out in more complex or less 'primitive' cases.

In an economic system where no bank exists, the circular flow of income becomes completely 'self-managed' by the economic subjects composing the system, leaving no room, in this way, for any expansion or contraction of the income produced in it.

However, in an economy *with* a banking system all the fundamental features of credit taking place between man and man disappear. The banking system, it is supposed, works like a 'filter' for the saving of the society.

In this way, granted the hypotheses given at the beginning, the direct communication between entrepreneurs and savers is broken off while at the same time the loan *market* is suppressed.

The money rate of interest is not a *market* rate of interest any more but a rate *fixed* by the banking system. It cannot work as a coordinating mechanism between decisions to invest and to save. The mediation set up by the banking system between entrepreneurs and savers implies now a different type of mediation for coordination, since now the connection between the two rates is 'much less simple' (Wicksell, 1906, p. 194) than before:

> The two rates of interest still reach *ultimate* equality, but only after, and as a result of, a previous movement of prices. (Wicksell, 1898b, p. 135)

In this quotation the situation of the economy with a banking system is concisely represented: the equality between the two rates is possible (there always exists, as before, an equilibrium which can be reached); this, however, is *not* automatic: to the 'objective' market mechanism is contrasted in parallel a 'subjective' one which the banking system can move at will. The 'signal' to variations in the *bank* rate of interest in one direction or another is given by the movements of prices which *must* take place as a condition for the possible correction put forward by the banking system through the interest rate policy.

The equilibrium situation characterised by the equality between saving and investment, a natural rate equal to the money rate of interest and by a constant level of prices, is now uniquely a *latent* reference whose effectiveness rests upon the characteristics of the actual economic system observed. There always exists, in other words, in the case now under discussion, a value of the rate of interest which *if* it were adopted by the banking system as a money rate would equalise the purchasing power of the saving to that of 'money' borrowed to finance the investment, but now the 'mechanism' leading to that situation is *no longer* embedded *inside* the scheme – as it was in the case where credit was negotiated between man and man. Taking for example the case of credit expansion, the latter will be financed by the whole saving set up by society *as well as* by that 'created' by the banking system itself, by means of the *non-*equalisation, for which the latter is ultimately responsible, between the money and the natural rate. Put another way, it is possible for the credit expansion to be *higher* than that allowed by the saving handled by the public. The circular flow of income, then, can experience either a contraction or an expansion according to whether the rate of interest set up by the banking system happens to be higher or lower than the natural rate (and as long as the difference persists).

The change in the terms of comparison adopted by Wicksell – non-monetary and monetary economy in *Interest and Prices*, economy with and without banking system in *Lectures II* – does not lead to substantial revision in the analysis of the cumulative process. It simply leads to a change in the emphasis of how the non-equilibrium analysis is presented, or much more precisely of the possible transition from this position to that of equilibrium.

In *Interest and Prices*, starting from an equilibrium situation without money, the conditions permitting the non-alteration in the economic system after having introduced money are analysed.

In *Lectures II* the analogous picture is given, starting from a situation which *normally* is in equilibrium (credit between man and man) in order to subsequently reach a situation which in general is not, because of the existence of the banking system. This is so because no automatic 'mechanism' is operating which would make it possible to cancel any possible difference between the natural and the money rate of interest: the 'equilibrium' position is uniquely a *reference* position and not a *convergence* position also.

2.9

In the discussion of the Wicksellian scheme the constant reference was the phenomenon of *inflation*, as the case of variations in the general price level. It should also be noted that the theory so far discussed can also be extended to the opposite case of *deflation*.

In this respect one has followed in the steps of Wicksell, who devotes to the second phenomenon hardly more than a few pages, inviting the reader to interpret the deflation case by turning the implied movements 'upside down'.

The symmetry of the two phenomena, in the analysed scheme, can however present some weak points. In considering inflation it is 'reasonable' to suppose that the changes in the monetary magnitudes – in terms referred to above – appear *before* the corresponding quantity movements; an effective expansion, as has been seen, is either excluded or deferred to a logically and temporally subsequent phase, which remains out of the reference scheme. In the opposite case, that of deflation, it is 'less reasonable' to suppose analogous quantity movements *after* those of the monetary magnitudes. An intuitive reason for that lies in the fact that for expansion a creation of *new* commodities, which do not exist, is needed, whereas for contraction it suffices not to produce goods in the same quantities as before.

Wicksell himself recognises this obvious asymmetry in the functioning of the system when discussing deflation and does not deny

> that there may be a *more or less permanent*, though not progressive, loss of employment by some of the workers – the industrial reserve. (Wicksell, 1898b, p. 149; italics added)

However, at the same time, he does not believe that his scheme –

exclusively devoted to explain variations in monetary magnitudes – can *also furnish* an explanation of movements in the quantities produced and employed in the economy. To this end he seems inclined to refer to a 'business cycle theory', in which the particular phenomenon of unemployment can much more conveniently find an explanation (Wicksell, 1906, pp. 208–14; 1907b).

NOTES

1. With such an hypothesis the possibility of considering banks on the same footing as firms is excluded. They on the contrary represent a particular institution whose role and functions rest defined not *a priori* but on the basis of the relationships emanating from the dynamics of the economic process. As an example of banks reduced to the same footing as firms – though in a different framework – see C. Panico (1980).
2. These two characteristics can in general *not* happen at the same time; cf. A. Leijonhufvud (1981, pp. 155–6).
3. The basic idea of that can be traced back in an essay of 1802 by H. Thornton (1939, pp. 253–4).
4. The natural rate of interest in Wicksell's terminology cannot be confused with the natural rate which Marx (1972) refers to. 'The average rate of interest prevailing in a certain country,' Marx writes, sharing Massie's opinion (1750), 'cannot be determined by any law. In this sphere there is no such thing as a natural rate of interest in the sense in which economists speak of a natural rate of profit and a natural rate of wages' (Marx, 1972, p. 362).

    Moreover, one does not accept the opinion of J. M. Keynes (1936, p. 243), who makes the natural rate identical to 'the rate of interest which will preserve the *status quo*'. In Wicksell one does not find any allusion in this sense.
5. The first case is relatively simple to treat. Here, in fact, the supposed equality between demand and supply of each commodity will not induce any movement in the respective market prices, and therefore current prices will be supposed the same in the future, or at least in the next period.

    In such a circumstance, market prices being equal to their production costs for every commodity, the natural rate of interest of each commodity will be equal to that of any other, and therefore there will be a *unique* natural rate in the system.
6. If, for example, one takes as a reference an economic system in expansion, in this case an increase in saving necessary to make capital accumulation possible can be seen as a relative diminution in the demand for consumption goods and, at the same time, indirectly, a demand for production goods relatively higher than the corresponding supply. In fact, the process of 'diversion' from one type of production to another

'presupposes an adaptability and a degree of foresight in the reorganization of production which is far from existing in reality' (Wicksell, 1906, p. 193).

In a market economy, thus, it is extremely probable that the economic system will be found 'not prepared' for an expansion in equilibrium, for there do not exist, by definition, mechanisms assuring, at the right moment, that *decisions* of saving be equal to those of investment.

7. In the case of capital accumulation, now under discussion, there will therefore be a multiplicity of 'natural rates' (in particular, those of production goods for which demand is greater than supply, will be relatively higher than those of the consumption goods the demand for which will be less than supply); in this case relative (market) prices cannot be assumed constant.
8. See also, B. P. Adarkar (1935, chs 6,7) and M. Desai (n. d).
9. See also, L. L. Pasinetti (1980–1).
10. The latter situation is the one which will happen in general and therefore the 'natural rate of interest' must be necessarily thought of as *an average* of those natural rates, corresponding to those commodities entering the definition of the general price level.

If then the system is supposed to be expanding it will be always possible – as Sraffa has pointed out in the discussion on Wicksell – to adopt as a 'money rate' the chosen average of the natural rates, so that the purchasing power of money saved can be made equal to that of the additional money required for investment (see P. Sraffa, 1932, p. 51).
11. Wicksell always maintained as rigorously distinct the two notions of money and natural rates of interest, from a strictly logical viewpoint as well as from an 'operative' one. See Wicksell (1906, p. 457) for some qualifications, and G. Cassel (1932, pp. 501–2) and L. von Mises (1934, pp. 357–64) for a critique. The latter reduces substantially the money rate as 'derived' from the 'real' one. Against such an interpretation, see J. A. Schumpeter (1954, p. 1118) and R. Frisch (1935–6, pp. 104–5). An explicit reply to such a critique is contained in Wicksell (1919, p. 251).
12. Wicksell's reference is to be found in K. Marx (1974, p. 119).

3 Wicksell's Elaboration: Some Preliminaries

3.1

Most of the literature dealing with Wicksell's monetary theory has interpreted it from a different viewpoint from that of Wicksell – as will be maintained in the present work. Moreover, that literature has quite frequently had a highly critical attitude, sometimes hostile, toward a theoretical approach which, in retrospect, can surely be taken as a milestone in laying the foundations of modern monetary theory.[1]

Both for method and content, the Wicksellian approach had to reveal itself more and more disruptive to a theoretical tradition having as its stronghold the 'quantity theory of money', which almost to the end of the last century was the most accepted theory. This latter judgement can be maintained in spite of the fact that that theory was increasingly becoming much less fruitful and hardly enlightening with respect to the great monetary (but not only monetary) upheavals taking place in that century.

At the same time it should be emphasised that Wicksell's contribution – relative to the field considered in the present work – is fundamentally devoted to the more general understanding of the basic mechanisms of the economic system (which was a capitalistic one at the time of Wicksell) and of its 'laws' underlining the phenomena characterising its development. It seems in fact apparent that those problems defined approximately as 'monetary' cannot be avoided by capitalist economies and that moreover they should be considered but a 'superficial' as well as a necessary expression of those much more profound from an economic-political point of view. On the one hand, this led Wicksell to investigate further the significance of some analytical categories and operative tools; on the other to give an unprejudiced interpretation of the capitalist reality which was ultimately the very object of his research.

What has been said so far, even if briefly, is decisively reflected in the interpretation of Wicksell's monetary theory here given. The intention is to give a key-reading quite different from those commonly accepted. To this end it seems necessary to start from a brief analysis of Wicksell's viewpoint. This in turn will lead to a discussion of some essential characteristics of a 'monetary' economy and its most immediate problems. This will be the object of the present chapter.

3.2

The main purpose which seems initially to direct Wicksell in his enquiry concerns an extremely concrete problem always present in the economic history of all countries: that pertaining to variations in the exchange value of money, i.e. its purchasing power.

The occasion or the intellectual curiosity for Wicksell of entering the monetary field is based on the endless controversies at the end of the last century, mostly technical than anything else concerning the simultaneous use of two parallel monies (gold and silver) in the regulation of commercial trade.

In his study he was bound to come across the still existing controversies relative to the quantity theory of money which, at the time Wicksell is referring to, had already accumulated as many opponents as had been their supporters.

The first Wicksellian writing on the subject dates back to 1897 (Wicksell, 1897).[2] The immediately following work of 1898 (Wicksell, 1898a) and, in the same year, his fundamental *Interest and Prices* (1898b) initially faced the problem mentioned above, namely the exchange value of money and its variations. In his *Lectures II* (1906), given the characteristic of this text, a short but important *Introduction* soon points out some fundamental features relating to an economy in which *systematically* the use of 'money' is taken into consideration. It will be useful to quote extensively the passage referred to:

> We have hitherto [in *Lectures*, vol. I] considered production, distribution, and exchange as if they were effected without the assistance of money, as if labourers, landowners, and capitalists received an apportionment of the product in kind. . . . This simplification of the problem is absolutely necessary in a preliminary treatment of economic phenomena, because actual economic life is usually too complex to be examined directly with any chance of success. It is also permissible – as a first approximation – because there can be no doubt that, in many cases, transactions which are

made with the assistance of money can be conceived as having been made without its intervention. Among the many similes which have been employed to illustrate the nature and functions of money that which describes it as the oil in machinery is, from many points of view, the most appropriate. Oil is not a component part of a machine; it is neither a motive force nor a finishing tool; and in an absolutely perfect machine a minimum of lubrication would be required. Naturally, however, our simplification is only provisional. Economists frequently go too far when they assume that the economic laws which they have deduced on barter assumptions may be applied without qualification to actual conditions, in which money actually effects practically all exchanges and investments or transfers of capital. (Wicksell, 1906, pp. 5–6)

Side by side with the characteristic of 'oil for machines' – taking into account the qualification above mentioned – Wicksell emphasises the *conventional* character of 'money' which makes it appear as an 'abstract symbol, a mere quantity of value' (Wicksell, 1906, p. 19) as well as differentiates it quite substantially from all other commodities. 'Money,' Wicksell writes, 'is a quantity in two dimensions, quantity of value on the one hand and velocity of turnover or circulation on the other' (ibid). All these things 'may appear simple and even trivial, though in nine cases out of ten they are forgotten when reasoning about money' (ibid). Thus 'money' in fulfilling in the economic system all the normal functions stops behaving like other commodities.

He points out carefully these differences. First of all the laws of exchange regarding common commodities cannot be extended also to money. Let us take the case of a seller offering commodities on the market: one can safely say he is demanding money; vice versa for a buyer. However one *cannot* affirm that *on the whole* society is demanding or offering a determined physical quantity of money, which in any case is incapable of being the final object of transactions. There does not exist, in other words, a determined relationship between the physical quantity of money and the volume of exchanges, since theoretically any quantity of it would be sufficient – given a suitable velocity of circulation. The expressions 'demand' and 'supply', then, once applied to money become 'obscure and, in reality, meaningless' (ibid, p. 20).

These remarks lead us to consider more closely the phenomenon of exchange in relation to 'money' or, more generally, the kind of relationships between relative market prices and money prices.

The exclusive function of 'money' as a medium of exchange becomes essential when more than two commodities enter the market in order to be exchanged. By supposing exchanges taking place simultaneously, in such a way that in the end every subject leaves the market *after* having been both seller and buyer, then the role of 'money' stays confined to that of intermediary and the exchange values formed thereupon for every commodity must be traced back exclusively to 'production and consumption conditions' relative to the commodities themselves. Any general price level will be compatible with the set of established exchange values. If on the supposed competitive market the well-known adjustment mechanisms are operating, then there always exists the possibility for 'wrong' or 'disequilibrium' exchange values being re-established as those which are 'right' or 'equilibrium' values.

In this connection it makes no difference in the substance if we assume, more realistically, exchanges taking place non-simultaneously in any given period, and that as a consequence, for example, a seller does not immediately become buyer (he will leave the market without having bought anything): he will hold his 'money' in order to make future transactions. Even by considering, together with the previous, the latter function of 'money' – that of being a store of value – there cannot spontaneously emerge *from the market* conditions regulating prices expressed in money. 'If there is any reaction whatever away from a *general* level of prices that is too high or too low, it must originate somehow or other from *outside* the commodity market proper' (Wicksell, 1898b, p. 24); more precisely one has to refer to the *relationships* between that market and the money market (ibid).[3]

Relative market prices and money prices are then situated on two widely separated and distinct planes. One important question which arises is, then: what are the different effects that variations of the two sets will produce for the community and what degree of 'social' control can one respectively have over both of them?

If relative market prices have as their reference base the 'production and consumption conditions', variations in the latter imply variations in the former, though it is difficult to say, without detailed and specific hypotheses, what sort of advantages or disadvantages can be produced for each class of individuals – at least in a relatively short period of time. So, for example, one of the effects of technical progress in one or more industries reflects itself in changed exchange values, but a punctual analysis in terms of 'costs and benefits' (in short) appears quite difficult to do. On the other hand, a 'social' control on the causes of variations here under discussion in a direct and immediate way is as hard to imagine. This difficulty becomes exacerbated if one considers the fact that with *relative* prices even an imperceptible and trivial variation in the production of a single essential commodity implies complex chain-effects over all other prices. Of course changes in relative prices will induce reactions by the economic subjects, though such reactions, as well as the causes, will take place in the long term, during which other events will probably occur to 'reshuffle' all the data of the problem.

In contrast, the effects of variations in money prices, or more concretely in the general price level in one direction or another, are much more clear for single groups of individuals, although in a contrasting and differentiating way; and, what is more, a given variation can be voluntarily *caused – within well defined limits –* by the subjects of the system, in ways and forms we have discussed previously. This should not be surprising if one reflects upon the fact that money prices are ultimately based on 'pure convention, depending on the *choice of a standard of price* which it lies within our own power to make' (Wicksell, 1898b, p. 4).[4] And more generally:

> with regard to money, everything is determined by human beings themselves . . . the choice of a measure of value, of a monetary system, of currency and credit legislation – all are in the hands of society, and natural conditions (e.g. the scarcity or abundance of the metals employed in the currency, their chemical properties, etc.) are relatively unimportant. (Wicksell, 1906, p. 3)

3.3

In considering some issues relative to the elaboration of the Wicksellian scheme, with which we are occupied at the moment, two more at least deserve particular mention.

These consist of two basic hypotheses adopted by Wicksell in his scheme: the first given by formulating a *pure credit* system, the second by explicitly considering a *closed* economic system – the latter much more general to that of an open system, since Wicksell is referring to the world economy as a whole.

With reference to the hypothesis of pure credit, 'a purely imaginary case' (Wicksell, 1897, p. 232), it simply consists in the assumption of neither metallic money nor banknotes in commercial transactions, which are instead regulated by simple book-keeping at the central bank of the system. Under these circumstances the 'velocity of circulation' of the medium of exchange is theoretically infinite and in addition the concept of 'supply of money' loses much of its significance; this is so not so much because 'money', meant as coins and banknotes, is trivially excluded by hypothesis; the point is that that supply cannot be given autonomous existence without at the same time referring to 'demand'. The latter, inasmuch as it is going to be expressed, creates itself a corresponding 'supply': a sort of Say's law reversed.

The case of pure credit does represent the opposite side of pure money, though even the latter, as the former, is an imaginary case. There seems never to have existed (even at present) actual economic systems having exactly those requirements pertaining to each of the two cases. In reality one can find the characteristics of both, though historically there always existed a tendency (not constantly uniform) of a prevalence of the pure credit.

One may ask why Wicksell – at the time he was writing of course, that is, between the end of last century and the beginning of the present one – was making use of that hypothesis – which was quite new in the economic literature. He justifies the inclusion of it in his theory simply in these terms:

> If one could get a clear understanding of the principles determining the purchasing power of money and the commodity prices in both of the standard cases, it seems to uncover the right solution of such a problem under the present circumstances. (Wicksell, 1897, p. 232)

Holding the opposite view, Ohlin interprets the Wicksellian hypothesis as a tool to escape from 'the tyranny which the concept "quantity of money" has until recently exercised on monetary theory' (Ohlin, 1936, p. xiv). It does not seem, however, that Ohlin's interpretation is correct.

Instead, one can trace an implicit motive as to why Wicksell came to formulating that hypothesis, based on the observation of the degree of 'development' which capitalism had so far arrived at: granted the huge volume of transactions necessary in the work of the system at the highest possible levels, there is no doubt that the bounding-up of the medium of exchange to an almost fixed quantity of 'money' (both coins and banknotes) should reveal itself insufficient in securing the increasing rhythm of commercial affairs; so that the system, though not creating, should at least stretch to the maximum the most convenient form for its development. 'In the development of society,' Marx noted, by referring to the historical form of money, 'not only the symbol but likewise the material corresponding to the symbol are worked out' (Marx, 1973, p. 145).

The Wicksellian hypothesis can thus be considered as a formidable methodological device as well as the breakthrough theoretical expression of a historical tendency of capitalism in order to understand the ultimate consequences of the working of the latter – within the bounds of the theoretical scheme of reference.

As regards the hypothesis of a 'world economy', here too Wicksell tries to bring – in analogy with the previous case of pure credit – to the extreme consequence the reasoning made on the causes determining variations in the general level of prices.

The hint was offered by Nasse, who ten years earlier than Wicksell had maintained that the *ultimate* cause of prices variations rested on the international shipment of precious metal, between countries, as a consequence of variations in prices inside a country due to credit policies, either tight or easy. However, Wicksell states (1897, p. 233, and 1898b, pp. 77–9) that if the prices of one country depend on those of others (this is the conclusion one arrives at following Nasse's reasoning), the question of what is the cause of variations in the general level of prices is simply transposed from a single country to others linked to the first by commercial relations. So the problem is only removed – not solved.

Also in this connection the scheme offered by Wicksell constantly makes reference to the hypothesis of a 'world economy', thus singling out one of the main features of a capitalism going towards an ever-increasing process of integration. In this way in analysing the monetary features of an economy he moved the emphasis to a higher and more general level.

In interpreting the basic Wicksellian scheme, one has to constantly bear in mind these two hypotheses – which usually fail to appear even in the recent literature – as well as to consider that the results obtained by Wicksell cannot be immediately 'applied' to reality, for he explicitly thought of the two cases as limit-cases, reality being *always* between them:

The monetary systems actually employed in various countries [referring to the hypotheses of pure credit and pure metallic money] can then be regarded as *combinations* of these two extreme types. If we can obtain a clear picture of the causes responsible for the value of money in *both* of these imaginary cases, we shall, I think, have found the right key to a solution of the complications which monetary phenomena exhibit in practice. (Wicksell, 1898b, pp. 70–1)

3.4

As we stated at the beginning of section 3.2, the main purpose of Wicksell's enquiry was centered on the purchasing power of money and its variations; as a consequence he was bound to deal with the thorny problem of price-index. In *Interest and Prices* he devotes the whole of chapter 2 to it, and subsequently in Lectures II a large section.

He first of all points out the stringent conditions necessary to make unambiguously . . . a comparison of the purchasing power of money at two different points of time. And even in this case:

> though there may be one general force operating on all prices in the same direction, calculated to bring about a perfectly uniform change, other forces usually come into play, arising out of the constantly changing conditions of production and consumption, and these must result in a different system of relative prices. The final result is shown in a somewhat greater rise in the prices of some commodities than of others, sometimes indeed in a fall in the prices of one or more groups of commodities when all other prices rise. (Wicksell, 1898b, p. 7)

He eventually affirms that 'a real solution of the problem is and will remain an impossibility' (1906, p. 136). It is clear that since one has to refer somehow to an 'average' one must constantly take into account the 'purely conventional significance' (ibid, p. 137) of it.

Side by side with these 'technical' difficulties another should be added. Any 'average' of prices having an economic meaning uniform for society cannot exist at all; 'its meaning cannot be the same for different individuals and classes of society' (ibid).

From what has been said so far a problem can arise, which was clearly put forward by Sraffa (1932, p. 51). Sraffa, in defending Wicksell from the adverse criticism of Hayek – in a way which will be evident in the next chapter – points out the *multiplicity* of price levels which alternatively one could choose to stabilise at any given moment. The possibility of having more than one single price to stabilise is the only 'objection' that can be raised against Wicksell. This 'objection', however, is an external criticism to his theoretical scheme.

Sraffa's remark, on the other hand, hides something very important: it posits again the problem – explicitly discussed by Wicksell, though in a different way – regarding on *whom*, for *whom*, and *how* a price-index can be built up, and thus focuses on the non-neutrality of this operation. Therefore in speaking of 'neutrality' with regard to monetary policy the overall 'weight' which can be attributed to it must be evaluated in the light of that remark. After all, Wicksell seems to be aware of that problem, devoting a great deal of attention to the issue in general – though a reviewer of this work seems to underestimate the importance of the issue, inasmuch as he maintains that it is 'not advisable to puzzle the reader with questions about the geometric or harmonic means, when the use of index numbers is only subsidiary to the main purpose of the book' (Sanger, 1898, p. 385).

NOTES

1. But on a different note see R. Frisch (1952), although M. Blaug (1968, p. 633) cooly defines his article as 'obscure' without offering any explanation.
2. One could perhaps say that, beginning with this work, Wicksell embarks on an analysis in which the role of the banking system is crucial, whereas in his previous work (Wicksell, 1896) that of the State is determinant.
3. One should note that this distinction does not imply that 'money' has no effect on relative prices.
4. See also, Wicksell, 1898a, p. 68.

4 Wicksell's Elaboration: The Making of the Scheme

4.1

In comparing the formal structure of Wicksell's treatment of the 'theory of production and distribution', on the one hand, and 'monetary theory', on the other, one thing appears quite evident: the very different methods adopted in tackling and exposing the respective problems of the two theories. As regards the former, Wicksell arrived on the scene at a time when three separate strands of thought, quite different from each other in approach, had just replaced that of the classical economists: (i) English marginalist, (ii) Walrasian, (iii) Austrian (Böhm-bawerkian).

There did not seem to be much scope for Wicksell (who, one should note in passing, started studying economics quite 'late' after training in mathematics (see T. Gårdlund, 1958, chs 4, 5)) to rebuild a theory on completely new foundations. As a matter of fact he tried first to investigate the compatibility among these strands of thought, to go more deeply into the results, mainly analytical, at which they had aimed, and to point out, neatly and without prejudices, their weak points. The 'first impulse', as he expressed it himself in his first systematic studies of the subject, consisted in fact in presenting 'the fundamentals of the modern theory of value and of Böhm-Bawerk's theory of capital' (Wicksell, 1893, p. 17).

4.2

Both in the field of the theory of production and distribution and in monetary theory, Wicksell's starting-point is classical theory, in particular that of Ricardo, for whom he always reserved a particular 'scientific respect'. The introductory part of *Value, Capital and Rent*

> consists of an attempt to evaluate the classical theory of value as it left Ricardo's hands – its merits, especially when compared with

Wicksell's Elaboration: The Making of the Scheme 49

the later theories of the 'harmony economists' and the socialists, and its defects. At a time when it has almost become a fashion to speak of Ricardo in disparaging terms, it may be permissible to emphasize once again the unquestionable merits of this acute thinker. (Wicksell, 1893, p. 17)

However, if his *starting*-point was the same for both theories, the *development* of each took profoundly different paths.

The development into the two fields had been, up to the time Wicksell was writing, quite unequal. In different ways and according to the various countries in which bad or good luck supported the progress of the theories, the three strands of thought were already well known and, at the same time, they effectively represented an alternative to the classical approach.[1]

But in the field of monetary theory nothing of that sort happened. At the time Wicksell was writing the only classical theory still standing was the 'old' quantity theory of money; in spite of the fact that it had been heavily under attack and criticised, nonetheless it had not yet been 'replaced' by any other – as had happened for the classical theory of production and distribution. As we saw in Chapter 1, Wicksell himself was careful to point out the fragile scientific solidity of all those theories which in different ways aimed at being alternative to the quantity theory.

This being the case, and considering the great shortcomings of the quantity theory, it is understandable that it was relatively 'easier' for Wicksell to set up his *own* theory of money, alternative to the dominant one. In fact he found himself more free to operate in the theory of money since without a doctrinal structure, generally accepted as that represented by the three strands of thought referred to above, he could be his own man.

It should then have been natural for Wicksell to 'broaden' or to 'apply' the marginal method, which he deeply analysed in other parts of economic theory, to monetary theory as well. After all, Walras made such attempts (cf. Walras, 1954, lec. VI; and 1886). But it was not so. Wicksell firmly criticised those attempts:

> It is true that many of the well-known workers on the theory of value, such as Jevons, Walras, and Menger, have entered fairly deeply into questions concerning money. But their treatment of such questions runs, for the most part, in the old ruts. For instance, Walras' exposition consists fundamentally of nothing more than a

mathematical version of the quantity theory which will be discussed below: there is no substantial development or extension of the theory itself. (Wicksell, 1898b, p. 18)

And what is more, beyond any statement, it is the concrete development as well as the basic structure he gave to his scheme which turned out to be in sharp conflict with the method of enquiry of the marginalist school.

4.3

Wicksell's research, as has been said, was fundamentally addressed to singling out the complex of conditions leading to variations in the exchange value of money.

One can certainly state, as a first approximation, that the exchange value of 'money', as any other value exchange, ultimately coincides with the 'price' at which it can be obtained, that is with the money rate of interest.

If one rigidly followed the quantity principle one could affirm that a 'low' money rate leads to increasing prices, and a 'high' rate to decreasing ones. More precisely this can be expressed in the following terms: putting P for the price level, then obviously $1/P$ is the part of the basket which can be obtained by one monetary unit, that is $1/P$ is the 'relative price' of 'money' measured in terms of its purchasing power. As a consequence, and strictly following the quantity theory, if an increase in the supply of a commodity provokes a diminution of its own relative price in terms of all other commodities (*ceteris paribus*), in the same vein an increase in the supply of money reduces its own relative price, $1/P$, that is the price level increases.

There would exist, therefore, for the three magnitudes so far considered the following symmetry: 'plentiful' quantity of money – 'low' money interest rate – 'high' money prices; and vice versa.

However, the synchrony of the movements, relative to the above magnitudes, is firmly questioned by Wicksell, both from the theoretical point of view – because one cannot explain the movement in the price level by exclusively having regard to what is taking place on the side of 'money' and disregarding at the same time what is happening on the side of 'commodities'; as well as from the empirical point of view – since statistics of price movements and money interest rates show that high rates remain associated with high prices, and not vice versa, as the quantity theory would lead one to conclude (Sauerbeck, 1895; Tooke, 1844, chs 12, 13).[2]

Let us investigate how the problem is settled in the Wicksellian scheme.

Wicksell initially introduces 'monetary' variables into an economic system by taking as a reference point a single subject, either seller or buyer. It is thereafter supposed that in an otherwise *unchanged* market situation *an easing of credit* takes place through a lowering of the money rate of interest.[3]

Naturally, a given diminution in the money rate of interest can produce different consequences for any single firm. Actually there can be found activities

> to which a rise or fall in the rate of interest is of very little consequence, since an expansion or contraction of their activities is prevented by technical considerations. It is equally true that there are many other businesses in regard to which such an occurrence is the decisive factor. Some enterprises are in a state of complete preparation; for others the plans for expansion have long been ready, and their execution only awaits a favourable opportunity; in yet others business is bad, and it is being debated whether they shall be carried on or closed down. In all such cases an easing or tightening of credit may be the last drop which causes the vessel to overflow, so that the plans which have been worked out are brought into execution. It is impossible to conceive that to-day, when almost every enterprise works on borrowed capital of one shape or another, it should be a matter of *complete* indifference whether the need for credit is at 3 per cent or 4 per cent, or only at 6 or 8 per cent. (Wicksell, 1898b, p. 89)

If for any single firm a given variation in the money rate of interest can have different consequences, for the economic system as a whole it is most likely that any variation of that rate is sufficient, whatever be its size, for a corresponding variation in money prices to be produced in the opposite direction. All that is necessary is the maintenance of the *ceteris paribus* conditions of the scheme, save of course the hypothetical reduction in the rate of interest; therefore 'unless the fall in the rate of discount is neutralised by simultaneous changes elsewhere, it must . . . provide a stimulus to trade and production, and alter the relation between supply and demand of goods and productive services in such a way as necessarily to bring about a rise in all prices' (Wicksell, 1898b, p. 89).

At the end of the period in which the easing credit conditions have taken place one can ascertain a level of money prices higher, on average, with respect to the previous period.

The conventional characteristic of money prices is such that, if all the effects of the easing of credit have been displaced themselves altogether, the new level of prices forms the base for all the economic calculations. The banking system even if it brought the rate of interest to the level immediately before the easing, nonetheless it would not be possible by this only to bring the new price level back to the former. And, if the easing of credit would be maintained in the immediately following period, then the price level will be still higher.[4]

4.4

In the reference scheme – so far considered in the most elementary form – one has generally discussed *single* money rate of interest. In reality, however – as is well known – there exists a multiplicity of rates as well as distinct classes of rates according to duration.

Wicksell took into consideration along with the banks – the latter seen prominently in their function of lending at short term – the stock exchange too, as the institution associated with long-term loans.

But the attention Wicksell paid to the banks as the 'heart and centre of modern currency system' (Wicksell, 1906, p. 73) should be regarded as much more than – indeed, in a different way from – a simple hypothesis historically based on an institutional feature pointing to the fact that the stock exchange did not have that 'weight' which it later came to have inside the financial institutions as a whole.

The banking system is able to create 'money' – and this is what Wicksell especially needs for his purpose. In such a system the economic power exerted through the management of money and credit, even if in different ways, must have an elasticity and a readiness to act which in no economic system, especially the capitalist one, can be left to the play of 'free forces' of the market. Certainly the 'interdependence' among different sectors, groups and classes of the economy makes for a non-one-way banking management and especially for a non-constant 'active' function of it.

A consequence of this well-justified emphasis is that the money rate of interest, referred to in the above reasoning – and subsequently – must be considered as the 'bank' rate, as distinct from the 'financial' one, contained in long-term credit contracts, typical of the stock exchange – though obviously between the two a link must be assumed to exist over the period considered. What, in other words, is here assumed is the hypothesis that the two rates are at the same level, for

> otherwise entrepreneurs would run their businesses on bank credit – this is usually feasible, at any rate by indirect means. Similarly it cannot stand lower than the short-term rate, for otherwise most capitalists would prefer to leave their money at the Bank (or to use it in discounting bills of exchange). (Wicksell, 1898b, p. 75)

4.5

Another aspect, among those which can be put forward from now on, is that regarding 'speculation'. Wicksell's enquiry is devoted to the study of what governs the exchange value of money whenever the system is *not* subject to irregular and peculiar movements which might hide the primary causes. In order to explain those movements further hypotheses are needed, or perhaps different ones from those made in the simple scheme of reference where a 'regular' functioning of the system was required.

Speculation in commodities – as distinct from Keynesian speculation in bonds not considered by Wicksell due to the exclusion of the stock exchange from the beginning – is certainly taken into consideration; but its action is designed to produce effects exclusively in particular periods of 'crisis'. Under these latter circumstances it would no longer be sufficient for a slight variation in the money rate of interest to produce an appreciable variation in the general price level; on the other hand, inflation or deflation in 'exceptional' periods of growth (high tension on the market, recession and standstill in productive activities) must be discussed in terms of far more complex causes with respect to simple changes due to a banking policy on interest rates, either 'active' or 'passive'.

It is precisely at this juncture that Wicksell opposes his own theory to that of Tooke. The latter gives, in fact, a determinant causal role to speculation in explaining inflation and deflation processes (Wicksell, 1898b, p. 90).[5]

Speculative movements were deemed important by the Cambridge school (especially Marshall) in explaining price variations – this seems to mark a separation and differentiation between that school and Wicksell (cf. Uhr, 1960, pp. 214–15).

Speculation can of course be incorporated into the basic scheme, Wicksell states. However, one should change also the general framework of market expectation, and he fails to consider this state of affairs, being only 'concerned with the organic development of a regular movement of prices' (ibid, p. 98).

4.6

In these last annotations reference has been made to the state of expectations, on which most of the literature has dwelt at large; one can even say it has often been given an excessive and disproportionate emphasis (see Laidler, 1972; Bailey, 1976; Humphrey, 1976).

Let us examine briefly how Wicksell fits the problem of expectations into his own analysis and what kind of role he attributes to them.

Two separate cases may be considered. The first is related to a deliberate policy to 'regulate' the exchange value of money, according to which the movements in the general level of prices are somehow expected to move in one given direction.

This case is based upon an opinion that Wicksell rejects, for reasons presently evident, and according to which a continuously increasing movement of prices would act as a stimulus to economic activity. On this he remarks that

> if a gradual rise in prices, in accordance with an approximately known schedule, could be reckoned on with certainty, it would be taken into account in all current business contracts; with the result that its supposed beneficial influence would necessarily be reduced to a minimum. (1898b, p. 3)

And with irony he goes on:

> Those people who prefer a continually upward moving to a stationary price level forcibly remind one of those who purposely keep their watches a little fast so as to be more certain of catching their trains. But to achieve their purpose they must not be conscious or remain conscious of the fact that their watches are fast; otherwise

they become accustomed to take the extra few minutes into account and so after all, in spite of their artfulness, arrive too late. (ibid, pp. 3–4)

The second case related to expectations deals more closely with the working of the basic Wicksellian scheme.

If one takes as a point of reference the case of an inflationary cumulative process, it is natural to fit in the hypothesis of increasing prices *after* the process itself has had sufficient time to strengthen its recurring dynamics:

> When prices have been rising steadily for some time, entrepreneurs will begin to reckon on the basis not merely of the prices already attained, but of a further rise in prices. The effect on supply and demand is clearly the same as that of a corresponding easing of credit. (1898b, p. 96)

It is true, as Wicksell himself admits, that these effects could be much more enlarged, for the easing of credit concerns initially only borrowing firms, whereas after some period of increasing prices and expectation of their further increase 'almost every purchaser will be able to offer higher prices and every seller to demand them' (ibid, pp. 96–7). However, more realistically Wicksell continues, either of them would prefer a smaller but certain gain against a bigger but uncertain one (ibid, p. 97).

In the case of increasing price expectations – the latter based *on the experience* of continuously increasing prices over a significant period of time – if the easing of credit, initially set up by the banking system, should cease, the upward movement of prices would ultimately cease too.[6]

The inclusion of expectations, therefore, is certainly not posited in a rigid way by Wicksell – though one could say that he quite consciously attributes to them a generally subordinate role.

4.7

Another aspect of what has been said above is represented by the 'passive' attitude of the banks with regard to the interest policy relative to supposed variations in production and distribution conditions reflexed in corresponding variations in the natural rate. This factor of 'passivity' is explicity underlined by Wicksell (1906, p. 204). It must however be understood in a very precise sense. If the *primum movens* lies on the side of production and distribution – as the causal element of the difference between the two rates – it is clear that in this sense the interest policy initially set by the banks remains 'passive'. However, this 'non-acting' is at the same time a positive element which inserts itself into the dynamic process.[7] It continues to do so thereafter, in a second sense, for such policy in itself does not furnish immediately an automatic mechanism of adjustment.

On the one hand Wicksell emphasises – as already noted – the 'sluggishness' of the banks in the manoeuvre of interest rates, sluggishness which is due to a double series of circumstances linked, firstly, to the hypothesis of a closed economy (i.e. the world economy) forcing a responsive action to the changed conditions of production slower with respect to variations in these conditions and secondly to the fact that these variations are reflected directly or indirectly in tangible and immediate 'market' mechanisms, whereas for banking policy one cannot assert that.

All this finds a systematic place in what Wicksell concisely calls the 'routine' of the banking system – a term which would be improper had he attributed to it a meaning linked to a mechanical 'banking technique'. Indeed, as he observes:

> If it were a fact that such changes generally spring from the banks themselves; that, in other words, the latter quite arbitrarily raise or lower their rates without being forced to do so by market conditions, then there would certainly be reason to expect rising commodity prices after a lowering of interest rates, and vice versa. But this is apparently not the case. The banks are always more or less *bound* in their interest policy, and even if this policy presumably could, through common action on the part of the banks which is nowadays becoming more prevalent, move within somewhat elastic limits, yet there predominates in the field of banking, more perhaps than elsewhere, precisely because of the great sums at stake, a procedure built up upon custom and tradition, in a word – *routine*. It may, indeed, be said that the banks never alter their interest rates unless they are induced to do so by the force of outside circumstances. (Wicksell, 1906, p. 204)

On the other hand, however, Wicksell himself points out the elements necessary for a *potential* 'active' action of the banks which,

Wicksell's Elaboration: The Making of the Scheme   57

as will be shown in detail later, does introduce a valuable degree of 'openness' into the theoretical scheme.

After having refuted the propositions of the Tooke school, which considered monetary policy as simply having an action limited to exceptional or secondary cases, Wicksell asks:

> But, it might well be asked, does the power of monetary institutions over prices operate only in this direction? Is it not logically necessary to suppose that under suitable conditions they can exert an influence in the opposite direction – that is to say, that they can raise prices? And is it reasonable to maintain that this influence in either direction can only appear in exceptional circumstances, such as the extreme conditions presented by a crisis? Should it not rather be supposed that the banks' discount policy, or more generally their credit policy – no matter how it may be determined – is *always* exerting a certain influence on the level of prices, either maintaining or disturbing it? If so, is this influence to be regarded as confined within *narrow limits*, such changes in the general level of prices as actually occur being brought about by other forces? If so, what is the nature of these forces? Or is it a characteristic of the banks that their power is *unlimited*, so that in a pure credit economy they could bring about any desired rise or fall in prices by pursuing a uniform policy with regard to the rate of interest? Is it possible that we have here found the general cause of the price fluctuations which occur under present conditions, when it is becoming more and more usual for instruments of trade and credit to pass through the hands of the banks? Does it follow that the most powerful instrument for stabilising prices lies in appropriate regulation of banking policy? (Wicksell, 1898b, pp. 79–80)

The passage just quoted gives in a nutshell the programme which Wicksell intends to develop, the pivot of which lies on the banking system as an inevitable element of the economic system. It contains also the seeds of that indissoluble interlocking 'triangle' made up by production, distribution and money or, as improperly referred to in more recent times, 'real' and 'monetary'.

Another testimony to such an interlocking aspect, partly pointed out above, is that 'money' cannot absolutely be seen as a middle link, or indeed as a simple *form* assumed by 'real' magnitudes.

As money enters into the productive circuit it becomes, on the same footing as other magnitudes, a determinant element. Here the feature, fundamental in the Wicksellian scheme, that everything *cannot* happen at once becomes crucial. It must necessarily pass through phases of the economic circuit each of which has its own task to carry out. Wicksell seems on principle not against the idea that the level of money interest rates is ultimately regulated by 'real' factors. But to try to get immediately to this, without going through the circuit, would conceal an important link over the sequence of the economic events. 'Money', in fact, does have a well-determined function as soon as it is lent – although at first sight it does not apparently possess a so straightforward connection with the other 'real' factors.

Here lies the source of his aversion to concepts that view interest as a 'remuneration for the use of capital and not for the use of money' or the loan of money as a 'loan of capital goods' (Wicksell, 1898a, p. 83; 1898b, p. 108 and p. xxvi).

Granted this complex interweaving, it should be possible to establish 'transparent' links among the principal magnitudes of the reference scheme – that is, the natural rate, the money rate and the general level of prices. In reality, however, it does not turn out to be like that. In fact, of these magnitudes, the first does not find any *tangible* expression in current economic relationships, as do the latter two. Therefore its existence and its variations in the economic system have to come into being by means of other variables.

4.8

In *Interest and Prices* a comparison is put forward between an economy without and an economy with money. Wicksell is very anxious to emphasise the fact that in a system where loans take place *in natura* and at a rate of interest which emerges from productive conditions, the general level of price cannot be subjected to movements either upward or downward.

The possible introduction of 'money', and consequently of loans made and expressed in money terms (that is, in an abstract unit of account in the case of pure credit), does not produce any substantial change in the elements describing the situations so far depicted. That introduction should be considered, as Wicksell himself says, in the same way as a 'cloak to cover a procedure which, from the purely formal point of view, could have been carried on equally well without it' (1898b, p. 104).

This situation does not bring in itself any particular difficulty. However, if instead of assuming an equilibrium system one considers a system *in transition* from one equilibrium position to another and in which therefore the plurality of natural rates necessarily imposes the need to make an average of them, the comparison between a situation *without* and another *with* money makes it lose the very distinction between a non-monetary and a monetary economy.

This essentially depends on the fact that the chosen *average* among the natural rates (and correspondingly the basket of commodities chosen as a reference to express the average level of prices) is *not* unique. Thus in this case, in contrast to the former case in which *any* commodity adopted as a standard would give the same result, it is necessary to choose *a* basket of commodities among the many possible. It is only *after* having made this choice that the Wicksell proposition could be valid according to which the adoption of *any other* standard could reproduce the same results as the former – that is, to leave unchanged, over the period considered, the purchasing power of the chosen basket.

In fact, if this *other* standard were 'money' (or the arbitrary unit of account in the case of pure credit) the comparison between the two economies, distinct on the base of the adopted standard, could certainly be made. The proposition according to which the *money* rate equals the *natural* rate (this understood as an average of the different rates, weighted in the same way as are the prices of the commodities composing the chosen basket) would have meaning. Money would have the mere function of a veil to cover a procedure which in the same fashion would have been possible without it, in the sense of leaving unaltered the supposed conditions of the loan.

The latter statement, however, loses all its strength if one comes back to the premise on which it is built, that is the arbitrary choice of the basket. If in abstract one can single out a multiplicity of baskets and if each can legitimately fulfil the function of standard, the exact singling out of 'natural economy' to be compared with a 'monetary economy' is lost. This is so because each 'natural' or 'non-monetary' economy, having its own 'money' – i.e. the composite commodity chosen as standard – in terms of which debts and credits are regulated, would not be so much different from any other 'monetary' economy.

This 'fundamental objection' – as it could be concisely called – is attributable to Sraffa (1932, pp. 49–50). In a sense, however, the Wicksellian distinction discussed above can retain a limited validity;

after all, if it is true that the choice of the standard is arbitrary, one can take that choice as *given*, discussing *afterwards* the various implications in the proposed scheme. As a matter of fact, on this arbitrary choice of averages Wicksell promptly pointed out the problem of its limits, both on the theoretical level as well as on the empirical one, as has been seen before in the discussion on the general level of prices.

All these drawbacks could certainly constitute a powerful stimulus to completely dispense with the concept of the price level: on the other hand it is at the same time difficult to accuse Wicksell of not having made that decisive step. If it is true that his theory, at the time he was submitting it, could be called 'heretical', a theoretical framework in the monetary field that was not making use of the concept 'general level of price' would have sounded incredible, to say the least.

4.9

It should be also pointed out that the production scheme implicitly assumed in the previous considerations is of an extremely generic character. That is, in effect, what suffices for the Wicksellian scheme. It is therefore not absolutely necessary to think of it as a neoclassical scheme or more specifically a Walrasian one. There is no indication in this connection for refusing other and different schemes of reference. The Wicksellian scheme relating to a monetary economy is not at all 'marginalist', either in its method or its structure.

It is otiose, therefore, to ask whether the 'natural rate' of interest is determined by the marginal productivity or by the intertemporal preference. Wicksell himself, as regards the scheme taken into consideration in the present work, does not give any explicit indication on this matter. In the subsequent literature that notion has been so often made *identical* to that of 'marginal productivity of capital' (for example, Ohlin, 1936, p. xiii).

It is only in the English version of a lecture by Wicksell in 1906 for the economic section of the British Association that an allusion is made to the possibility of the natural rate being 'compatible with the existing marginal productivity of real capital' (Wicksell, 1907a, p. 216) – although, at the same time, the identification of the two concepts is not granted.

This can be partially explained by the fact that Wicksell had to use

Wicksell's Elaboration: The Making of the Scheme 61

the language of the English economists of that time, which, as is well known, was completely dominated by the Marshallian doctrine. It is unfortunate that Ohlin – it should be observed with irony – in the 'Obituary' on Wicksell, published in the *Economic Journal*, does not think that the 1907 essay 'does Wicksell full justice. His style, usually vigorous and stimulating, is here rather heavy' (Ohlin, 1926, p. 507).

NOTES

1. It is worth noting that Wicksell expressed some doubts on the internal consistency of the neoclassical theory of value, although he was unable to draw any conclusion. See Wicksell (1901, pp. 185, 191–206); also P. Garegnani (1960, ch. 6); A. Bhaduri (1966); L. A. Metzler (1950); S. Brusco (1976).
2. See also J. R. T. Hughes (1968).
3. From the standpoint of a seller paid through a bill of exchange at a fixed date, that corresponds to cashing a greater sum than he would have cashed without the easing of credit; from the standpoint of a buyer, alternatively, one might suppose he buys with borrowed money, so that a lowering of the money rate of interest puts him in the position of paying a higher price than that which he would have paid without it.
4. This is the well-known 'cumulative process'.
5. See T. Tooke (1844, pp. 81–2). See also Wicksell (1907b).
6. There seem to exist some analogies between this Wicksellian position and that of Keynes. On Keynesian expectations, see T. Lawson (1981, especially pp. 313–14 and 317–18).
7. For this same reason one could also maintain that it is also potentially 'active', in the sense that by basing themselves on a discretional element the banks could move the money rate of interest at *any* moment, to *any* direction and with *any* rapidity of adjustment. This, however, remains *outside* the analytical framework here under discussion.

5 The Orthodox Interpretation

5.1

Soon after the Second World War a revival took place in the analysis of the foundations of monetary theory, which had its peak, after several articles, in the well-known work of Patinkin, *Money, Interest and Prices* (1965). This work is of the utmost importance for the topic here considered: it contains in fact an interpretation of Wicksell's monetary theory, summing up in an extremely clear way many other interpretations, which all follow – Patinkin's included of course – a certain and definite viewpoint (as well as a certain and definite 'vision' of the economic system) concisely centered on the notions of 'equilibrium' and 'stability' of equilibrium.[1]

Patinkin's interpretation of Wicksell is explicitly formulated in chapter 8 of the above work, meaningfully entitled 'A Critique of the Neoclassical Theory of Money' (together with Note E on 'Wicksell's monetary theory'). In order to better understand Patinkin's *interpretation*, which is of interest here, it is necessary to make reference to other central parts of his *analysis*, for the two are not at all disjoint. Patinkin himself emphasises this in his Preface to the first edition of his book.[2]

It will be shown later that not only is Patinkin's interpretation of Wicksell's monetary theory quite different from what has been attempted in Chapters 2–4, but also, and especially, how much that interpretation is indissolubly tied up with the *type of analysis* or framework underlining it.

Patinkin addresses himself, in the above work, mainly to the problem of 'integrating' value theory and monetary theory.[3] It would seem obvious, then, that one of the problems to be specified in advance will be that of deciding *which* value theory and *which* monetary theory have to be 'integrated'. To this end it does not seem necessary to enter into the details of Patinkin's book to get an answer to that problem; for the value and monetary theories he intends to integrate are from the very outset specified respectively as the Walrasian theory of general equilibrium and the quantity theory of money.

First of all, the 'scenery' he assumes in his economic system is typical of the neoclassical tradition: the subject is, according to the case, the individual and the community (this latter intended as an aggregate of economically isomorphic individuals); the object being the 'goods' fundamentally divided into the two groups, 'commodities' and 'paper money'.

The link between *that* subject and *that* object is given by the 'market', which seems to be the only place where it is possible to express and analyse – following the strand of thought which Patinkin is referring to – the 'economic' functioning of the system. It should be noted from now on that the apparent simplicity of these hypotheses will produce irreversible effects over Patinkin's entire construction, particularly in the working of the 'monetary forces'.

'Money', in fact, is represented as a physical entity on the same footing as commodities; as a 'good' it will be subjected to the same principle governing commodities, save of course for the case that '[m]oney buys goods' but 'goods do not buy money' (Patinkin, 1965, p. xxiii).

The action of each and every individual is aimed towards the acquisition of 'goods' to be determined 'optimally' in the sense of a well-defined constrained optimisation problem. Furthermore the economic aspects providing the background against which the 'constrained optimisation' takes place are the forces emerging from exchange relations taking place on the market.

In order to address attention to the way in which, in this reference scheme, 'money' is introduced and the consequences of its introduction for the economy as a whole, it would be useful to look into some of the details of Patinkin's reasoning (ibid, ch. 2).

In a simple barter economy any individual will enter the market, as a buyer or seller, only if he expresses an *excess* demand for goods, respectively positive or negative (which is the difference, respectively positive or negative, between quantity demanded and initially owned).

The excess demands and supplies depend on the current system of market prices, and the real value of endowment of goods initially owned by the subject (real income). But the very existence of those excess demands, in the 'scenery' above depicted, is strictly connected with an *automatic* mechanism for their elimination such that not only can an 'equilibrium' be represented – in which, that is, every excess demand (positive or negative) is equal to zero – but also especially that one can always get to the equilibrium.

A crucial point arrived at is, namely, the assumption of an

equilibrium for the system – as specified above – and of its attainment, which presupposes or sets the scene for *stability* of equilibrium. Before analysing this point, it is important to pose briefly the question of what happens inside the system once money is introduced.

The introduction of money, into the simple exchange economy so far considered, or indeed its existence as a component of the whole 'wealth' owned by every individual at a given moment, is based on the fact that now, in contrast to the previous barter system, exchanges take place only by means of money (which is thus a medium of exchange): moreover they do *not* take place all at once, so that every individual will decide to hold a given amount of money as a store of value. How much each individual will want to possess will naturally depend upon a set of both objective and subjective factors related to the problem of synchronisation between 'expenditure' and 'income'; but the very important point to stress is that the adequacy of 'real balances' will be judged on the basis of the quantity of commodities they will obtain in the market. Thus, in contrast to the barter system, the excess demand for a commodity expressed by each individual will depend not only on relative prices and real income, but also on the *real* value of the quantity of money initially owned, that is on 'real balances' of cash.

The introduction of such an argument into the functions of excess demand constitutes the 'crucial' element in Patinkin's analysis. The 'wealth' owned by every individual will thus consist of two components: commodities *and* money, both valued in *real* terms. Then, as before, a hypothetical variation in the endowment initially owned produces – *ceteris paribus* – a variation in the quantities of goods demanded; now, in addition, a hypothetical variation in the quantity of money – *ceteris paribus* – will produce a corresponding variation in the quantities demanded – and this is the well-known *real balance effect* (Patinkin, 1965, p. 19 and fn. 13). Such an effect, then, can be assumed to take place through a variation in the quantity of money possessed by any single individual as well as through a proportional variation in all the commodity prices.

By means of the introduction of money into the economy, alongside the functions of excess demand for every individual there will now be a place for an 'excess demand function for money" – whose excess will be given by the difference between the quantity of money one desires to possess at any given moment and the quantity of it initially possessed. In such a type of economy every individual intending to buy a commodity will have to finance it by drawing from

The Orthodox Interpretation 65

his endowments of either 'real balances' or commodities possessed, so that 'excess demand for money' becomes synonymous with 'excess supply of commodities'.

Thus, if an individual wants to change his proportion of commodities, he will also have to change in general his own amount of real balances, expressing in this way an excess demand for money (either positive or negative).

By supposing that the excess demand functions for commodities depend *exclusively* on relative prices and on the real value of wealth possessed – absence of 'money illusion', in Patinkin's words (1965, p. 24) – it follows that proportional variations in money prices, and at the same time in the quantity of money initially possessed, will leave unchanged the *real* value of the quantity of money demanded by any single individual.[4]

5.2

Given the outline of the essential characteristics of the scheme into which money has been introduced it is now necessary to draw attention to the functioning of the economic system as a whole, which – as has been said above – will be limited to the determination of equilibrium prices *and* their stability.

As recalled before, an equilibrium position will be defined by the fact that all markets will be 'cleared',[5] which means an excess demand for every commodity equal to zero; which in turn is necessarily equivalent to saying that the excess supply of money is zero. More generally, if for the $n-1$ goods of the system an equilibrium position exists, this necessarily implies an equilibrium position also for the nth good. It should be noted that commodities and money are the 'goods' considered; the nth good (thus the nth market) can be *any whatsoever*. This is essentially Walras's law. The latter allows, equivalently, that of the n excess demand equations, only $n-1$ are independent, and therefore a set of equilibrium prices satisfying the $n-1$ equations will satisfy at the same time the nth equation too (Patinkin, 1965, pp. 15–17, and appendix to ch. 3).

Having sharply distinguished money prices from accounting prices, one can deduce, from what has been said, that to the determination of the $n-1$ money prices will correspond the indeterminacy of the n accounting prices. The *practice* of choosing only the price of money as the accounting price should not hide the *analytical* fact pointed out above, to which Patinkin draws particular attention: namely, the analytical fact of considering money on the same footing as any other good.[6] Money prices, in fact, are prices – like the relative prices of commodities – which are determined *on the market*; whereas the accounting ones do not possess this feature, for they, by definition, are *arbitrarily* given.

Now one has to ask:

(1) how the market determines equilibrium prices;
(2) what characteristics 'market forces' possess to lead the economy towards an equilibrium position.

As to point (1), the determination of equilibrium prices rests on the well-known Walrasian process of *tâtonnement*, on which one need not dwell. It should be noted, however, that it has not been by chance that the characteristics of this very procedure have been the core of some of Patinkin's critiques with special reference to the Keynesian system (cf. Clower, 1965; Leijonhufvud, 1969, 1968).

What we are mainly concerned with here is point (2). In this connection Patinkin himself notes the profound difference between the assertion 'that the process of *tâtonnement* prevents the market from remaining at a non-equilibrium set of prices and even exerts some sort of pressure in the direction of equilibrium', and the statement 'that this process must ultimately bring the market to the equilibrium prices themselves' (Patinkin, 1965, p. 39).

Patinkin is of course highly interested in the latter case taking place. In effect, this is exactly what happens in the 'system' as it has been made up.

The feature of the market forces in the system are such that any non-equilibrium performance is *automatically* suppressed. This can be clearly seen from two standpoints. In one it is supposed that the *ratios* of money prices proclaimed by the auctioneer be different from those of equilibrium; in the other it is supposed that the *absolute level* of money prices be different from that of equilibrium.

In the first case the 'substitution effect' will be at work, making for an increase (decrease) in the prices of those commodities showing an excess demand (supply) – since the corresponding relative prices are higher (lower) than the equilibrium ones.

In the second case, on the other hand, the *real balance effect* operates: the very fact that the *real* value of money balances is by hypothesis different from the equilibrium level will produce demands

The Orthodox Interpretation   67

(or supplies) over the various markets and correspondingly pressure on price towards the direction of equilibrium.

In both cases, therefore, market forces will be automatically generated in order to get the system to an equilibrium position. One should note in passing that the distinction made above is uniquely related to the *effects* of the working of market forces and not to the separate working of two markets (the commodity and the money market): in effect both relative prices and money prices are simultaneously determined by market forces (Patinkin, 1965, pp. 43, 181).

5.3

It is now necessary to analyse Patinkin's interpretation of Wicksell's monetary theory.[7] For this purpose it will be useful to first point out the ultimate goal which Patinkin does want to achieve by means of his own 'integration' of monetary with value theory. This 'integration' fundamentally consists in giving rigour and in completing the quantity theory of money, which the tradition (both classical and neoclassical) had left full of gaps and logically self-contradictory.

According to Patinkin, then, the theoretical elaboration over the quantity theory of money, both in the 'cash balance' and 'transaction' versions, had resulted, in different ways and in different degrees of consciousness, in the formulation of the following fundamental aspects (Patinkin, 1965, pp. 163–4):

(1) given an optimal relation between the level of cash balances and the expenditure of every individual, a hypothetical increment, e.g., in the quantity of money, 'disturbs' such an optimal relation;
(2) the effect of such a disturbance will consist, in the supposed case of an increase in the quantity of money, in a corresponding increment in the volume of expenditure of each individual – *real balance effect*;
(3) that increment will push upward the level of prices till the point at which it has increased in the *same* proportion as the quantity of money has increased.

Now, the tradition of thought is inadequate, according to Patinkin, for not having pointed out and systematically incorporated into the analysis the 'crucial intermediate stage' (ibid, p. 165) mentioned in point (2) above – that is, that a variation in any single expenditure is the effect of the dropping of the optimal relation between this and cash balances as a consequence of a variation in the quantity of money. And this is the pivot around which Patinkin's entire construction turns. Of this construction there are two essential aspects which deserve to be emphasised for the development of the issues considered: one is relative to the *function* that monetary theory should, according to Patinkin, fulfil; the other concerns the *modes* of development of the mechanisms inside the theory. The two aspects, then, are strictly connected and both necessary to define one's conception of the economic system.

5.4

Let us begin with the first. After a brief consideration of Patinkin's framework, outlined in the previous section, it is clear that *the* economic problem stated there was essentially that of determining the exchange ratios between goods, or more precisely the set of 'equilibrium prices'. 'Money' cannot be an exception; on the contrary, a necessary condition for an 'integration' between it and the 'real' side of the economy, made in a rigorous and coherent way, does indeed require a complete assimilation of money itself into the ranks of commodities, in the sense of its being exclusively considered as having the functions of a medium of exchange and store of value. For commodities, the problem is that of determining their relative exchange ratios – i.e. the field of value theory – and for 'money' the analogous problem is that of determining the absolute level of money prices. It is therefore *this* which is the main function of Patinkin's monetary theory, and from what has been said so far it appears evident that the integration between the two theories – value and monetary – must resolve itself into the complete absorption of the second theory by the first. Monetary theory therefore is distinguishable from the more general (neoclassical) value theory by the identification of its own object – which is money – as well as by the effects produced in the economy deriving from hypothetical variations of it. However, both theories – as previously noted – by having as their goal that of determining 'equilibrium prices' *cannot* be distinguishable by their mode of operation: both relative commodity prices as well as the absolute level of money prices must be simultaneously determined.

If that is true – as Patinkin shows – there no longer exists, then, the

The Orthodox Interpretation 69

dichotomy between value theory on the one hand and monetary theory on the other. The presence of such a dichotomy, in fact, is the basic charge he makes to the traditional classical and neoclassical thought in the monetary field; that dichotomy is responsible for leaving in the air the determination of the absolute level of money prices – which, as has been said, is the very function monetary theory has to perform. Actually if one assumes a given initial position of equilibrium, uniquely disturbed by a proportional variation of *all* money prices, it does not change with regard to relative commodity prices, so that the markets of these will continue to remain in equilibrium even after that hypothetical disturbance. By Walras's law, therefore, the money market will remain in equilibrium too. This fact, then, will mean that in the economic system no excess demand is produced such as to make money prices return to the original position. Thus the conclusion is that if a set of money prices is in equilibrium, any multiple of that set will be in equilibrium as well, which means that the absolute level of money prices is indeterminate (Patinkin, 1965, p. 43).

This 'indeterminacy', it should be underlined, was certainly not considered a weak point by the supporters of the quantity theory of money; indeed – as Patinkin himself reminds us (ibid, p. 175) – it was believed to be a necessary assurance of the characteristic element of the theory itself: variations in the quantity of money bring their effects on prices but not on quantities. Since money had to be *neutral* with respect to the 'real' side of the economic system, a necessary condition of that was believed to be the complete independence of demand functions from the absolute level of money prices. However, as Patinkin shows, it is this very 'independence' which feeds back against the theory itself, since the latter by making the *real balance effect* non-operational does not assure the full development of the process after variations in the quantity of money have taken place. On the contrary, once that dependence is admitted, the neutral feature of money emerges in a non-contradictory way.

As to this first aspect of Patinkin's analysis – that is, the function monetary theory has to perform – the conclusion seems to be that once it is restrained in the determination of the absolute level of money prices, it is *ipso facto* included within the more general theory of value.

5.5

Let us now turn to Wicksell's involvement relative to the aspect so far considered.

Although Patinkin considers Wicksell as belonging to the neo-classical strand of thought, he at the same time points out various differences between him and that strand (Patinkin, 1965, note E, secs 1, 2, 3).

These differences turn out to be the gist of the critique Patinkin makes of the supporters of the quantity theory of money, who left this theory in a state of profound uncertainty, due mainly to the presence of the dichotomy discussed above.

In order to test how little solidity such an interpretation has, let us review those differences, already mentioned, and put forward by Patinkin. This will emphasise how Wicksell did recognise the *real balance effect* and the process through which the absolute level of money prices is determined.

The passage Patinkin is referring to for his thesis, fully reproduced in a special 'appendix' (ibid, pp. 581–2), does indeed contain the idea of the *real balance effect* but, at the same time, it does *not* make it the pivot for the determination of the absolute level of money prices. In this case, in fact, he believes that there is some hope of seeing the *real balance effect* at work. In this case the quantity theory of money would be confirmed in its most characteristic aspect, i.e. the stability of the equilibrium position.

It should be noted here that the passage under discussion is inserted in *Interest and Prices* within the chapter relative to the quantity theory, in which Wicksell formulates in full his own criticism against that theory, both from the theoretical as well as the empirical standpoint, by concluding in the following way:

> The Quantity Theory is *theoretically* valid so long as the assumption of *ceteris paribus* is firmly adhered to. But among the 'things' that have to be supposed to remain 'equal' are some of the flimsiest and most intangible factors in the whole of economics – in particular the velocity of circulation of money, to which in fact all the others can be more or less directly referred back. It is consequently impossible to decide *a priori* whether the Quantity Theory is *in actual fact* true – in other words, whether prices and the quantity of money move together in practice. (Wicksell, 1898b, p. 42)

This is in its substance repeated also in *Lectures II*, under the section entitled 'The defects of the quantity theory. An attempt to a rational theory'.

In both these works – this is the point to stress – we are still far away in any sense whatsoever from the theory Wicksell wants to submit, and whose core is subsequently illustrated in the 'systematic exposition' which is found in chapters 8 and 9 of *Interest and Prices* and in the 'positive solution' of *Lectures II*.

It becomes then natural to ask Patinkin why Wicksell within his own theory did *not* develop the 'vital' parts of the quantity theory; and, in particular, why he did not incorporate in his own analysis the *real balance effect*. This refers immediately to the function which according to Wicksell monetary theory should perform. From what has been said in Chapter 2, relative to the theoretical scheme of a monetary economy, one is unable to conclude that the above function does coincide with that which Patinkin has in mind: it does *not* consist in the determination of the absolute level of money prices. According to Wicksell it is neither the central problem of monetary theory nor a problem of crucial importance in any case. Indeed, within his theoretical construction it does not exist as a problem.

This apparently paradoxical fact can only be explained by admitting a substantial difference between Patinkin's approach and the Wicksellian one. This difference is composed of various elements. First of all Wicksell was not at all interested in the *static* problem of the determination of the absolute price level but in the *dynamic* one, consisting in the periodical inflationary and deflationary cycles which had characterised and were still characterising different economies in the world. This urged Wicksell, as has been seen, to inquire *how* 'money' was entering the circuit, *to whom* it was flowing, and *by whom* or *by what* its 'quantity' could be determined.

This set of questions had, then, necessarily stimulated the analysis to break away from the homogeneous world made up of identical individuals characterising the Walrasian approach, and to assign the classes of the system the functions corresponding to the new problem put forward. Moreover the market cannot be the exclusive reference point of all the economic mechanisms; also the productive process had to be involved.

Besides, in order to investigate the phenomenon of inflationary and deflationary movements the function of 'money' both as medium of exchange and as store of value was evidently insufficient for the purpose, and 'credit' managed by the banking system should be systematically inserted. In the 'ideal' case of pure credit it is clear that once 'money' (now intended as a 'good' on the same footing as all other commodities) is eliminated, all its characteristics automatically collapse, as opposed to what happens in the Patinkin scheme; even though in the Wicksellian scheme one does not come back to a barter world, as would happen with Patinkin; instead one makes a step forward towards a configuration of an economic system much more close to reality, in which credit managed by the banks is thought to play a decisive role in the functioning of the economy as a whole.

As a support to what has been said so far, let us consider what Wicksell states at the end of his 'systematic exposition' of the theory contained in chapter 9 of *Interest and Prices*:

> Many of the above statements must, in their relation to the traditional treatment, appear almost paradoxical. . . .
>
> It might further be asked whether we are right in suggesting that it lies in the power of the credit institutions, acting in cooperation only with the entrepreneurs, to determine the direction of production and consequently the period of investment of capital, without paying any heed to the actual capitalists, the owners of goods. Here too there can be no doubt that this really is the case (though in practice this power cannot be so absolute as we are supposing). (Wicksell, 1898b, pp. 154–5)

The latter circumstance is made more clear by Wicksell by means of the case of 'forced saving'.

If the banks lend to the entrepreneurs for a period, say double that necessary for the production of consumption goods, this will mean that the correspondingly undertaken investments will come to fruition only at the end of the period concerned. At the half-way point of the period, then – that is, at the end of the 'normal' period of production – if the capitalists used *all* the capital deposited with the banks to buy consumption goods, this will uniquely result in an *increase in prices*, for the quantity of them ready for the market will obviously be less than that 'corresponding' to the entire capital – the difference consisting in that quantity of goods which will be ready at the end of the period relative to the loan initially given by the banks to the entrepreneurs. What happens, therefore, is an imposition on all the consumers for the exact amount of saving necessary to make that amount of investment possible.

The Orthodox Interpretation 73

This allows Wicksell to reach the following conclusion:

> These considerations are of extreme importance in relation to actual economic events, but they are usually overlooked in the customary treatment of the theory of money, being regarded as relevant only to a natural economy. (1898b, p. 156)

According to Wicksell, therefore, the case of 'forced saving' is not an exception to the norm, a special case; it represents on the contrary a case which takes place as a rule, as an effect of the existing relationships among the classes and the banking system with regard to the productive processes of the economy as a whole.

But according to Patinkin, the case of 'forced saving', which he refers to in passing (1965, pp. 164, 371), represents an 'exception', a 'disturbance' to the rule requiring that money resources be uniformily distributed among the subjects in order that uniform effects be produced by their variations, and to confirm through this route the validity of the fundamental thesis according to which 'money' is ultimately neutral. In the Patinkin scheme, in fact, where demand functions depend on the absolute level of money prices,

> in the new equilibrium position [after having doubled the quantity of money] the individual is confronted not only with a doubled price level, but also with a doubled initial holding of money. Hence – as compared with the initial equilibrium position – there is no real-balance effect; hence there is no change in behaviour; and hence the classical neutrality of money is reaffirmed. (Patinkin, 1965, pp. 175–6)

A profound and substantial difference then emerges between the two approaches, which, as far as the first aspect so far discussed is concerned – that of the function of monetary theory – shows quite evidently that that function, in the Wicksellian scheme, cannot possibly be reducible to the function emerging from the quantity theory of money following the version offered by Patinkin – that is, that of simply determining the level of money prices. However, posing *this* problem would mean at the same time disposing of, from the beginning of the analysis, all the complex of forces which lie at the back of the 'data' of the traditional approach (which is the quantity theory of money) – a complex of forces which should instead be the very object of the inquiry.

Wicksell points out the insufficiency of such an approach, based on his profound conviction that by that approach it is impossible to explain the real movements of the economy and that therefore one needs to break out of that theoretical framework and to build up a new one. Continuing to stay within the old framework was, according to Wicksell, to indulge in 'a mathematical version of the quantity theory' without any substantial development or extension of the theory itself' (Wicksell, 1898b, p. 18). That would have implied, however, the attribution of a new role to money in the process of exchange and production as well as the searching out of a new link between the 'money' market and the commodity market.

The circumstances according to which Wicksell does not fall into the trap of the 'invalid dichotomy' between relative and money prices (Patinkin, 1965, p. 586 and fn. 18) can thus be interpreted in two ways. In a trivial sense, he clearly distinguishes prices expressed in an abstract unit of account from money prices; it is in this sense that Patinkin interprets him, crediting to him a point in his favour against those erroneously falling into that dichotomy. But in a more subtle and substantial way that distinction seems to mean for Wicksell a warning not to mix 'money' together with all the other goods (neatly distinguishing in this way the money market from the commodity market) and to extract it from the 'mechanism' of regulations of commodities; this 'mixing up' would reduce – as actually happens in Patinkin – monetary theory to a simple subset of the more general neoclassical theory of value, whose function – as repeatedly said – is uniquely that of determining static 'equilibrium prices'. Wicksell was decidedly opposed to this, remarking that

> money prices, as opposed to relative prices, can never be governed by the conditions of the commodity market itself (or of the production of goods); it is rather in the relations of this market to the *money market*, in the widest sense of the term. (1898b, p. 24)[8]

From what has been said so far it is not surprising that Patinkin finds the above Wicksellian proposition 'uncomfortably obscure' (Patinkin, 1965, p. 587).

The valid dichotomy to be found in Wicksell is the fruit of his device consisting in *not* putting 'money' alongside all the other goods. This leads, then, to the need to consider more closely the way in which Patinkin must deal with the 'new' Wicksellian construction –

which he cannot ignore, but which he must interpret in line with all he was previously saying, including his own theoretical construction.

5.6

With this, we come to the second aspect of Patinkin's analysis, that regarding the *modes* of development of the mechanisms determining the 'equilibrium' variables. It is this aspect which is most important, since – as we shall see presently – through those modes the neoclassical theory can find a definite full expression. Patinkin writes:

> There is a basic chapter missing in practically all neoclassical monetary theory – the chapter which presents a precise dynamic analysis of the determination of the equilibrium absolute level of money prices through the workings of the real-balance effect. This is said, not for that aspect of dynamic analysis which describes the forces *propelling* the economy toward its new equilibrium position after an initial monetary increase – a problem adequately discussed by many neoclassical economists – but for that aspect which describes the forces *stabilizing* the economy at this new position once it is reached – a problem separated by just a nuance from the preceding one, but nevertheless discussed only by Wicksell. (Patinkin, 1965, p. 168; italics added)

This passage briefly outlines a very important side of Patinkin's contribution relative to the 'integration' between value and monetary theory, as well as – of somewhat direct interest – his position in 'allocating' Wicksell within that 'integration'.

The basic problem laid down in the passage quoted reflects the anxiety of the author for whom the static solution of the equilibrium position lies uniquely bound up with the determination of the price system or at most with the description of the possible forces acting towards the direction of equilibrium. In any case, one would leave the theory half-way. This means that, although the system is *potentially* able to get an equilibrium position (always definable), one can never say whether or not and when it can *practically* get that position. Were the matter this way, the neoclassical approach would leave monetary theory in a very unsatisfactory state: the 'harmonic' aspect of the functioning of the system cannot be maintained with rigour any more, and one would thus lose one of the most qualifying sections of the entire theoretical construction. This is reinforced by considering that within a barter economy the analysis is 'complete' both statically and dynamically: 'demand and supply forces' define in fact an equilibrium position and guarantee also that the system is always able to converge to it if by chance it strays outside. This is the reason why, according to Patinkin, the 'basic' chapter missing in the neoclassical theory extended to a monetary economy, concerns the working of the mechanisms *stabilising* the economy at the equilibrium position. Within his theoretical framework, as previously noted, Patinkin succeeds in tracing a dynamic process having the above property, which comes out through the working of the *real balance effect*. However, he goes further, by asserting that the problem has been discussed 'only by Wicksell', showing how this statement finds confirmation in the theoretical framework of the latter.

In what follows, then, analogous to the first aspect, an effort will be made to show that Patinkin's interpretation of the Wicksellian scheme – relative to the second aspect here discussed – is completely without foundation. In doing so one can also point out those innovating features of Wicksell's scheme which are in sharp contrast to the whole neoclassical structure.

The presence of a banking system having a discretionary power of fixing the money rate of interest is one of the features of Wicksell's scheme. But such a presence in an utterly uniform and compact Walrasian world of individuals and their behaviour, such as Patinkin's, does create worrying dissonances and asymmetries. The preliminary operation Patinkin has to carry out in order to 'homologate' Wicksell to his own scheme concretely reduces itself to that of adding an individual whose name is 'Bank' to the anonymous and undifferentiated individuals already present in the scheme, and attributing to it the *same* characteristics of behaviour as the latter; then to show that the reformulated scheme does correspond to the Wicksellian one.

Thus it can be understood how by means of this device nothing is substantially changed in the basic Patinkian scheme, and therefore the properties already shown valid for it would continue to be also valid for the reformulated 'Wicksellian' one.

The task of proving that such an operation cannot be accomplished in Wicksell turns out to be highly complicated, for one must trek through again with Patinkin an itinerary composed of a chaotic mosaic of quotations alternately derived from *Interest and Prices* and *Lectures II*; but nonetheless it is a task which has to be done.

The Orthodox Interpretation

However, as will be attempted in the following pages, that reconstruction is much like that of drawing from whatever book, the Bible for example, words or pieces of phrases in order to compose Pascal's thoughts. With patience and a suitable choice that is always possible to do: but it would not be possible to maintain that the Bible *contains* Pascal's thoughts.

Given the goal of assimilating the behaviour of the banks to that of any other individual, it seems necessary to endow the banks with 'cash balances' (which will assume the form of 'bank reserves') in order that variations of those – as happens to all other individuals in the system – will produce corresponding variations in prices. In this way the *real balance effect* is automatically extended to the banks, and the basic thesis of the quantity theory of money, through the working of that effect, remains thus reconfirmed. The role of the Wicksellian cumulative process, according to Patinkin, would simply be to put forward that fact:

> A correct appreciation of the place of the 'cumulative process' in Wicksell's monetary theory must start from the understanding that Wicksell always regarded himself as an adherent of the quantity theory and as one of its loyal defenders against critics. (Patinkin, 1965, p. 587)

Here Patinkin does not recognise one of the 'weak points' of the quantity theory of money among many pointed out by Wicksell, namely that the quantity theory of money 'assumes an almost completely individualistic system of holding cash balances' (Wicksell, 1898b, p. 41). He maintains instead that the 'collective' system, which contains the banks, can be seen just as an individualistic system *plus* the banks themselves.

At this point, then, he is bound to assume as a 'standard case' of the Wicksellian scheme (Patinkin, 1965, p. 589) that consisting of an open economy, functioning under the *gold standard*. It is uniquely in this case, in fact, that he believes that there is some hope of seeing the *real balance effect* working, thereafter confirming the quantity theory in its most characterising aspect, i.e. the stability of the equilibrium position.

We must now examine:

(1) how that 'standard case' works;
(2) whether that 'standard case' assures in general the stability condition;

(3) whether or not it is actually the 'standard case' analysed by Wicksell.

As to the first question, let us assume that trade takes place between two types of economies: one, economy A, produces gold, another, economy B, produces commodities. Starting from a position of equilibrium, both monetary (constant level of prices) and productive (equality between demand and supply), let us suppose that in economy A a new gold-mine is discovered. This will imply that a greater quantity of gold than before flows to economy B. This fact disturbs productive equilibrium and if the demand for commodities from economy A overtakes the supply from economy B this in turn will produce effects on monetary equilibrium, since prices will tend to go up. But *to whom* does the greater flow of gold go? There are two possibilities:

(a) it can go straight into the hands of the merchants of economy B;
(b) it can be transferred (even partially) by the capitalists (of economy A producing gold) straight to the banks (of economy B producing commodities) or indirectly by means of the merchants of economy B who deposit it at the banks.

By this, one comes to the second question. In the case in which the greater flow of gold follows the route under (a), the banking system never comes into play, which substantially means that its 'cash reserves' will not be disturbed by that flow and there will be no effect whatsoever on the money rate of interest; therefore there will be no *real balance effect* from the banks. If instead the route is that traced under (b), bank reserves will undergo an alteration. In order to put the greater quantity of gold in circulation (or equivalently a greater quantity of notes) the banks will have to fix a lower rate of interest.

By supposing the natural rate of interest unchanged, this will produce an increase in prices and the greater quantity of gold (or notes) will be consistent with the new level of activity. In such a case the excess quantity of 'money' in circulation does not exist and therefore the banks will be able to return to the original level of money interest rate.

It seems clear that *a priori* one cannot say which route the greater flow of gold will follow; it is also evident that only under case (b) will the phenomenon of 'excess bank reserve' be produced.

Let us check what Wicksell says on this matter. After having

The Orthodox Interpretation

pointed out that there are two causes for the commodity price level change – one related to the demand for commodities (from the economy producing gold) relatively greater or smaller than supply (from the economy producing commodities), and the other related to a money interest rate higher or lower than the natural rate – he maintains:

> It is not possible to subsume these two causes under a common cause (as I tried to do in my early work, *Geldzins und Güterpreise*, following Ricardo's example), since the quantity of money and the velocity of circulation of money are two different things, even if they both have an influence on the price level. Only in so far as new gold is deposited in the banks in the form of 'capital', i.e. without being drawn out in cheques and notes soon after, can it give rise to a lowering of interest rates and in that way affect prices. But this need not happen, and, contrary to Ricardo's view, does not happen as a rule. Rather most of the gold flows in in payment for goods and should then, in proportion as it exceeds the demand for new gold, have a direct influence in raising prices without lowering interest rates. Indeed, this effect may, . . . even precede the inflow of gold, in which case its influence on interest rates will rather be in the contrary direction. (Wicksell, 1906, pp. 215–16; italics added)

Wicksell then explicitly excludes that case (b) can take place as a rule. For Patinkin, however, it is this which is the most important case, for by means of this the *real balance effect* for the banks can take place. By an 'un-fair' quotation from Wicksell he tries to eliminate from the Wicksellian scheme the second cause for a variation in prices explicitly recognised by Wicksell and in this way to make case (b) the unique one. Thus Patinkin states:

> In his *Interest and Prices* Wicksell considers only the indirect effect, and so insists that no change in prices can take place without a prior change in the interest rate. In *Lectures II* Wicksell not only modifies this stand by introducing the direct effect, but goes as far as to relegate the indirect effect to secondary importance, stating that 'contrary to Ricardo's view, [it] does not happen as a rule' (*Lectures II*, p. 215). (Patinkin, 1965, p. 590, fn. 32)

Patinkin's quotation is clearly misleading: what in fact 'does not happen as a rule' is *not* the indirect effect, but the deposit of gold with the banks – as pointed out in the above quotation from Wicksell cited on purpose.

But the central problem of the second aspect here under discussion is expressed by Patinkin in the following way:

> Are there any forces which bring the cumulative process to an end? Do there exist any 'limits . . . which restrict the power of the banks' to maintain indefinitely a rate lower than the real one? (Patinkin, 1965, p. 591)

The two *distinct* questions Patinkin is asking give the impression of being two alternative ways of introducing the same question, whereas, on the contrary, they are referring to two *different* questions. In fact, the first one poses the problem relative to the existence of 'forces', that is of mechanisms already present in the economic system which are put in motion from the moment in which the cumulative process starts. The second question, instead, is referring to 'limits' within which the cumulative process takes place, without the intervention of 'forces' bringing a halt. Forces and limits, then, must be considered quite distinct. Patinkin, however, finding no answer in Wicksell to the *first* question – simply because it does not exist everywhere – makes it only the *second* question to follow, which subsumes the first one. Were the answer to the second question traceable in Wicksell, then – according to the approach of the problem given by Patinkin – one could conclude that the Wicksellian theory of the cumulative process contains 'forces' leading to a stop of it, and that therefore an 'instability' or 'non-equilibrium' phenomenon does have only a transitory or accidental nature. In this way the harmonic and equilibrating feature of a monetary economy would be confirmed.

In this connection one has to examine in which context of Wicksell's work the second question can be traced.

In chapter 8 of *Interest and Prices*, preceding the 'systematic exposition of the theory', Wicksell illustrates the conditions making for a continuous increase or decrease in money prices, by referring to the relationship between the natural rate and the money rate of interest. He subsequently asks 'whether it is possible for credit institutions to maintain their rates of interest at any desired level, or whether they are obliged sooner or later . . . to come into line with the natural rate' (Wicksell, 1898b, pp. 107–8). He points out:

The latter is the view generally held by economists. *In principle* they are perfectly right; but they usually omit to provide any clear account of the *manner* in which the two rates of interest are brought together. (ibid)

In the case in which a money rate of interest is by hypothesis relatively lower than the natural rate, thus money prices showing a continuous increase, the 'structure' of the money market is highly important to see *whether* and *how* the process can come to a stop, or, the two rates reach an equalisation. A 'market' reaction to an alteration of prices can only come out of a rather 'rigid' money market structure, in the sense often made explicit by Wicksell himself, which is concisely expressed by a rigidly given money supply which does not easily adapt itself to changes in demand. In the supposed case of increasing prices, the demand for money loans will increase with the need for 'cash', so that the money supply by becoming insufficient relative to demand will push the two rates to be equal. This is the case, however, in which the economic system works exclusively with a rather primitive credit system. But as long as the system acquires a credit organisation more efficient 'as a result of concentration in the hands of the banks of cash holdings and of the business of lending, and of the use of bills and notes, cheques and clearing methods' (Wicksell, 1898b, p. 110), money is rendered more fluid and the monetary system becomes then 'elastic'. The reaction to an alteration of prices becomes then negligible and 'a fairly constant difference between the two rates of interest could be maintained for a long time, and the effect on prices might be considerable' (ibid).

In the 'pure credit' case, it is then

> no longer possible to refer to the supply of money as an independent magnitude, differing from the demand for money. No matter what amount of money may be demanded from the banks, that is the amount which they are in a position to lend . . . it follows that the banks, or rather the aggregate of banks taken as a whole, can within limits to be stipulated in a moment lend *any* desired amount of money for *any* desired period of time at *any* desired rate of interest, no matter how low, without affecting their solvency, even though their deposits may be falling due all the time. It follows that if the rest of our theory is correct the banks can raise the general level of prices to any desired height. (Wicksell, 1898b, pp. 110–11; italics added)[9]

Here Wicksell emphasises the power the banks possess in determining the money rate of interest and thus – within his theory – in determining the movement of prices. The 'limits' he is referring to in the passage quoted, and which he will *subsequently* take into consideration, put the boundaries, in a non-rigid way, around the field within which that power is exerted – power which is still there and is not at all removed. What do those limits consist of?

In *Interest and Prices* he first takes into consideration the case either of a single bank or of the banks of a single country, noting that in this case an autonomous interest rate policy cannot be followed in a stable way, for it must take into consideration the analogous policy put forward by *other* banks. But in the case of a world economy reference to *other* banks is by definition excluded and the limits to the interest rate policy can be determined by two factors: one relative to the relation between consumption and production of gold, the other relative to the relation between quantity of circulating medium and bank reserves. As to the former, in the case of a money rate of interest fixed at a level lower than the natural one, and then with prices increasing more and more, a continuous diminution of the purchasing power of gold will induce an increasing consumption of it for industrial uses; the upward movement in prices persisting, consumption can overtake production and so induce withdrawal from bank reserves – the unique source at disposal. Bank reserves can also be drawn on – this being the second most important factor according to Wicksell – when a huge amount of gold-money (or notes representing it) circulates into the system compared with the amount of bank reserves; therefore an increase in prices could produce a drastic reduction of such reserves so as to induce the banks to raise the rate of interest. (Movements in the opposite direction would take place if the banks continued to maintain a rate of interest above the natural rate.) Wicksell, however, has doubts about the actual possibility of reaching those limits, in the light of experience, not least that regarding the consistency of bank reserves; in fact if it is admitted that 'the banks' reserves are unnecessarily large and could be diminished without endangering their solvency, it must also be admitted that the banks could lower their rates of interest still further if they desired to do so' (Wicksell, 1898b, p. 115).

Wicksell's reasoning on 'limits', however, does not end at this point. It goes on by clearly pointing out the premise from which it started, namely the fact that the 'economists' are excessively worried about establishing the ultimate attainment of those limits, and not about *if* and *how* those limits are actually attained:

It is confidently to be expected that the Bank rate, or more generally the money rate of interest, will always coincide *eventually* with the natural capital rate, or rather that it is always *tending* to coincide with an ever-changing natural rate. But whether this result is achieved with sufficient *rapidity* to prevent a continual rise in prices . . . or to obviate a gradual fall in prices . . . seems *a priori* very doubtful. (Wicksell, 1898b, p. 117)

In *Interest and Prices* this set of propositions substantially concludes the reasoning on 'limits', from which one could conclude that Wicksell contradicts what he was saying previously on the limits of banking policy. This would actually be the reading of the 'economists' whom Wicksell is referring to, Patinkin included, who omits to make direct reference to the reasoning contained in *Interest and Prices* (so far discussed) by preferring that of the *Lectures II* in which Wicksell, however, is much more sarcastic: that reasoning, in fact, is concisely contained in the last paragraph of the section concluding Wicksell's critique to various exponents of the strands of thought who were concerned with the problem of price movements and located immediately *before* the 'positive solution' contained in the *subsequent* section.

That apparent contradiction disappears as soon as one takes a different view from that of the 'economists'. This different view has as its starting point the fact that within the Wicksellian reference scheme *there does not exist any mechanism whatsoever* able to 'transform' a position of equilibrium to another one.[10] In other words, the 'economic forces' of the system cannot be assumed to operate in a linear and symmetric way; moreover one cannot ignore everything that happens from the beginning of a change in some economic variable and its concrete development, as if it were always and under any circumstance a transitory or secondary phenomenon. The alternating of inflationary and deflationary processes taken by Wicksell as a starting reference point as well as the object of his inquiry, was related to rather consistent periods of time. How could it then be possible not to ask what would have happened *during* the development of those processes?

To this regard the following often quoted passage of Wicksell draws particular attention:

Every rise or fall in the price of a particular commodity presupposes a disturbance of the equilibrium between the supply of and the demand for that commodity, whether the disturbance has actually taken place or is merely prospective. What is true *in this respect* of each commodity separately must doubtless be true of all commodities collectively. A general rise in prices is therefore only conceivable on the supposition that the general demand has for some reason become, or is expected to become, greater than the supply. This may sound paradoxical, because we have accustomed ourselves, with J. B. Say, to regard goods themselves as reciprocally constituting and limiting the demand for each other. And indeed *ultimately* they do so; here, however, we are concerned with precisely what occurs, *in the first place*, with the middle link in the final exchange of one good against another, which is formed by the demand of money for goods and the supply of goods against money. Any theory of money worthy of the name must be able to show how and why the monetary or pecuniary demand for goods exceeds or falls short of the supply of goods in given conditions. (Wicksell, 1906, pp. 159–60; italics added)

Wicksell's emphasis on the analysis of the economic *process* – in terms specified above – is clearly posed; and such an analysis will receive attention in the following chapter.

NOTES

1. Among these interpretations one can also include P. Garegnani (1979, pp. 63–82). As well as the similarity of the mechanisms of the functioning of Wicksell's monetary theory in both Garegnani and Patinkin – as will be shown throughout the present chapter – one has in particular to point out that Garegnani attributes to Wicksell 'the marginalist concept of interest as the supply-and-demand determined price of the productive factor "capital"' (p. 64).

   In this respect, however, the money interest rate in Wicksell, within the scheme comprising the banks, does not manifest itself on the loan 'market', but is *fixed* by the banks themselves. Secondly, Wicksell 'by real capital means real capital and not money capital' – as Sraffa had emphatically pointed out, in his celebrated debate with Hayek. Actually, Wicksell remarks, 'it is money which is lent, not the goods purchased by means of money. The rate of interest is a matter for negotiation with the owners of money and not with the owners of goods. The most eminent of

writers have contributed *very peculiar views* on this subject' (Wicksell, 1898b, p. 108). *Among these* one can include Ricardo, who had clearly affirmed that 'the rate of interest is not regulated by the abundance or scarcity of money, but by the abundance or scarcity of that part of capital not consisting of money' (Ricardo, 1951b, pp. 88–9). (The same is also confirmed, though in a different way, in his *Principle*: Ricardo, 1951a, p. 363.)
2. Among the authors to whom he expressed his intellectual debt Wicksell is mentioned: 'from the text the reader will likewise see how much my thinking has been colored by Knut Wicksell's classic *Interest and Prices*' (Patinkin, 1965, p. xix). (The preface to the first edition is reproduced also in the second one.)
3. The subtitle of his book is in fact *An Integration of Monetary and Value Theory*.
4. It should be stressed that this is valid for a *single* individual, since – as Patinkin remarks (1965, p. 33) – for the economy as a whole an increase (e.g.) in the quantity of money into the system could take place differently for each individual considered.
5. Compare this notion of equilibrium with that contained in F. H. Hahn (1973, p. 26) in which the characteristic defined in the text is absent.
6. Patinkin assumes that a solution exists, it is unique, and also economically meaningful (cf. Patinkin, 1965, p. 37 and appendix III). One has also to note that the system, referred to in the text, could also be expressed in a *form* such that no equation is eliminated: on this see Patinkin (1965, appendices II and III). In the latter case one can easily show that the system can at most determine *money* prices, that is the ratios between *commodity* prices and the price of money, all expressed in the chosen unit of account.
7. Here, he does two things at the same time. First, he includes Wicksell, together with economists like Walras, Marshall and Pigou, among the supporters of the neoclassical theory of money in the well-known 'cash balance' approach, with the important difference that the Wicksellian contribution rests on a 'perfection' of the quantity theory of money, in that Wicksell would have put forward, although incompletely, just those aspects which if coherently developed would lead to its validity. Secondly, he depreciates heavily the innovative part of Wicksell's theory in order to reduce it to his own and so make that theory consistent with his interpretation of Wicksell. The following will attempt to make clear the reason for rejecting such an interpretation, and to show that such a distorted image tends to obscure the main features of a theoretical effort that aims to oppose the traditional approach; cf. Patinkin (1965, p. 163).
8. One should note in passing that whenever Wicksell speaks of the money market he intentionally underlines, within his own scheme, the peculiarity of it with respect to others (non-monetary). For example, the Wicksellian banking market is formally very similar to a monopolist, but, contrary to the normal case, it does not have any objective function to maximise. Actually the Wicksellian banks do make a zero (net) profit, whatever the supply 'price' fixed by them.

9. In a letter to Umberto Ricci dated 17 July 1908, Wicksell restates the content of this quotation with the same clarity and determination.
10. For a contrary opinion, see J. Marschak (1941, pp. 476–7), F. Bruni, (1978, p. 610) and G. Scanagatta (1978, p. 136).

6 A Critique of the Orthodox Interpretation

6.1

In Wicksell's 'scientific programme' a vision of the economic system seems to emerge which precludes reading economic phenomena either in terms of 'equilibrium' or as a mere transitory phase; this should be understood in the sense that these phenomena can neither possess any precise meaning nor operate in unequivocal direction without at the same time making reference to the institutional and political relationships existing in the economic system considered. So the money rate of interest, for example, is *not* the outcome of 'free play' between demand and supply – as it would be in a primitive system of exchange taking place among individuals; it it *fixed* by the banks. The fact that the latter may *afterwards* change their decision is both possible and probable; this, however, will essentially depend upon 'external conditions' (Wicksell, 1906, p. 461), certainly not on automatic mechanisms already contained inside the system. There emerges then a new attitude towards economic problems. The kernel made up by the set of 'economic relationships' seems to be broken by the introduction of 'power relationships'. This remark is of a crucial importance not only for Wicksell's monetary theory but also for economic theory in general.

It is with neoclassical theory that political economy shows more and more evidently the tendency to attain its *own* autonomy, finding explanations for its *own* phenomena by means of its *own* 'laws'. This is achieved in the most trivial way by introducing automatic and objective mechanisms, which, working above individuals, always assure the outcome of the 'normal situation': the 'economic kernel' becomes then a *closed* kernel. In the Wicksellian scheme of monetary economy the 'kernel' is instead *open*. The fixing of a norm – which here means the fixing of a money rate of interest in line with the natural rate – is by no means assured: there does exist the possibility for that particular norm to be verified, but its concrete feasibility is entrusted to something else which the 'model' certainly does not explain, because it is not able to. This does not mean the scheme is missing something or is incomplete. If one prefers, it can be 'closed', but in an infinite number of ways. This essentially depends on the fact that 'power relationships', by their very nature, cannot be defined in a mechanical way. No 'law' therefore can assure that the banking system simply adopts *that* particular policy as to the rate of interest corresponding to an unaltered price level. This last position, in fact, is not the norm within the scheme; rather the contrary is true: the norm lies in prices alternately increasing or decreasing. The constant price level position itself has the role of being only a reference outside the scheme.

The 'analytical' reflection of what has been said so far can be traced back within the Wicksellian framework through at least two routes. First there is Wicksell's particular insistence on the continuous changes of the natural rate of interest (Wicksell, 1898b, p. 106) as opposed to a discontinuous variability of the money rate fixed once and for all by the banking system: hence the concept of 'high' or 'low' money interest rate in relative terms.

Second, one has to consider the hypothesis adopted by Wicksell in his scheme regarding the existence of 'pure credit'. What is the reason for the introduction of such an hypothesis? In addition to what has been said previously, according to the above hypothesis the banks are completely free from any curb restraining their freedom of action. There is no need to use quantities of gold as reserves, for there is no reason for these to exist; thus the supply of 'money' will not be subject to any restriction. The policy of determining the money rate of interest, therefore, can be considered in the first instance as not dependent upon any other 'monetary force'. The use of a discretionary power in the policy fixing the money rate of interest by the banks can be seen, in other terms, in its most transparent form.

The system of pure credit is a completely 'imaginary' case – as Wicksell himself states (1898b, p. 70). However, its introduction into the system gives an indication of the properties of banks' behaviour as well as the consequences of its working within the productive system, which otherwise would be somehow 'obscured' by the presence of proper 'money'. It is thus 'imaginary' in an analogous way, as Sraffa's standard commodity is. Even the latter, in fact, does not exist inside the real system under observation; nonetheless, starting from the productive methods in use one is always able to compose a system having determinate properties, and thereby to throw light on some features of the real system which otherwise could not be pointed out, even if they are already present. The standard commodity, then, is 'imaginary' only in its construction, but 'real' in its use.

Analogous consideration can be made for the imaginary system of pure credit – even in the different context of reference and *mutatis mutandis*. It is obvious that in any actual system one can always find *combinations* of 'pure credit' and 'pure cash'. But this 'mixed up' system, so to speak, is *not* a perfect blend of the two extreme cases: it always contains 'variable proportions' of the features belonging to either system. This essentially means that the 'constraints' imposed by the 'pure cash' system will not always be operating in the same fashion and under all circumstances; the same thing can be said regarding the 'freedom' of the 'pure credit' system.

In the Wicksellian scheme there does not exist any rule for which one can *a priori* establish a unique universal combination. Were this possible, it would then mean that 'economic relationships' would be such as to allow the possibility of representing beforehand the features of the movement of the economic system according to well given and rigid norms. At the same time it would also mean not recognising the necessary aspect of 'discretion' which characterises banking policy in this respect. But it is this very aspect which *is* a prominent and inevitable feature of the entire Wicksellian construction which allows 'power relationships' to enter in a determining way the development of economic affairs. Such relationships, by their nature, cannot be specifically detailed, which, however, matters very little: their systematic presence is of the utmost importance within the scheme. On the other hand, it would be naïve to believe in a banking policy exercised 'in a vacuum', for it necessarily must refer to the complicated network of relationships defined on the basis of the distinct functions of the social classes or groups inside the productive system: and vice versa, for the latter – as has been seen in the analysis of the theoretical scheme – cannot possess a self-determination which leaves out of consideration the presence of the banking system and its policy.

6.2

On the basis of this interpretation relative to a fundamental aspect of the Wicksellian scheme, it is then possible to attribute a precise meaning, too, to the 'passive attitude' which seems to characterise banks' behaviour, pointed out also by Wicksell.

Against possible changes of the several factors directly pertaining to the system of production, of which most are reflected in the extreme variability of the natural rate of interest, the banks can never have ready the most 'suitable' policy, since fundamentally the development of the various actions cannot take place according to rigid and automatic mechanisms which are known beforehand. As the natural rate of interest depends on 'all the thousand and one things which determine the current economic position of a community' (Wicksell, 1898b, p. 106) so the money rate of interest too has behind it a set of extremely different and complicated forces. An important difference between the two rates, as elsewhere noted, lies in the fact that the former does not show itself as a 'tangible' phenomenon, as opposed to the latter (cf. Marx, 1974, p. 432–7).

The banking system, then, becomes 'passive' in a quite distinct way. This 'passivity', however, is transformed by Patinkin into a state of 'ignorance' of the banks in the face of various movements to which the economic system is subjected, and consequently into a 'wrong' policy adopted by them.[1] And it is interesting to enquire into the reasons why Patinkin is led to such a belief.

The statistical trend of prices and the money interest rate shows that they are positively correlated, against theoretical expectations.[2] However, according to Wicksell's theory this does not appear as a paradoxical fact, for the level of the money rate of interest must always be correlated to the level of the natural rate. And as long as a difference exists between the two, prices will show a tendency to move. For Patinkin, then, Wicksell's interpretation of the well-known Gibson paradox is based on the fact that 'bankers never learn – even in the long run' (Patinkin, 1968, p. 124).

But what is it that the bankers never learn? According to Patinkin, it is the adoption of an interest rate policy which *returns* the system to the monetary equilibrium path, and thus to a constant price level. The prolonging over time, even over long periods, of inflation and deflation would then be due to a 'long term ignorance' of the banking system, which remains 'passive' in the face of various phenomena.

At the basis of such an interpretation lies Patinkin's conception of the 'dynamics' of the economic system: the equilibrium path is not only a reference path, it is also a convergence path. It must then represent the norm. As a consequence, inflation and deflation must represent transient phenomena, as a link between states of equilibrium. If, then, the statistics of the events show the opposite trends, the persisting state of disequilibrium could not be due to anything but the banks' 'lack of learning' to move in the right direction – only in

A Critique of the Orthodox Interpretation 91

this way, in fact, do inflation and deflation remain 'frictional' phenomena.

Under such circumstances it is easy to understand why for Patinkin a 'pure credit' economy appears as an uncomfortable case, finding no place in his scheme, for in that kind of economy – as we have seen on numerous occasions – reserve constraints limiting banks' action within determinate limits become by definition insufficient and at the same time are tangible signals to move unequivocally in this or that direction. It is not surprising that Patinkin asserts that Wicksell's pure credit hypothesis is 'restrictive' – since it is asserted in order to make his own scheme as close as possible to Wicksell's (Patinkin, 1965, p. 595).

Within the Wicksellian theoretical scheme the 'pure credit' hypothesis not only exists but it constitutes, in addition, the standard-case – in opposition to what is maintained by Patinkin. The 'pure credit' hypothesis, in fact, is not a limiting one but, on the contrary, it allows Wicksell to put forward the very nature of the economic power of the banks. In such a context posing the problem of 'stability' of the economic system becomes an idle exercise.

The cumulative process in Wicksell, in fact, is neither stable nor unstable. This follows from the fact that the path defined by the monetary equilibrium conditions has the *unique* function of a *reference* path *and not also* of a *convergent* one – which is the case in Patinkin. What for the latter is a norm, for Wicksell, on the contrary, is simply an abstract possibility. The non-equilibrium *is* the norm, for in the theoretical scheme there exist no mechanisms which make convergence automatic to stabilise the system at a state of 'equilibrium'.

It appears, then, that Wicksell's position is completely reversed by Patinkin's interpretation, a reversal which is based on the two authors' different conception of 'dynamics' and which refers more generally to their different vision of the economic system considered. The theoretical picture offered by Wicksell using the 'pure credit' case makes a breakthrough in the analytical apparatus of traditional economic theory, according to which the *ultimate* explanation of any phenomenon whatsoever must be brought back *inside* the theory. Any region of indeterminacy which eludes the working of 'economic laws' is then seen as an anomaly or a freak case.

Patinkin cannot be persuaded, for example, that the banks *can* be in a position to produce *any* price level by means of their adoption of a money rate of interest different from the natural rate. His method of reasoning forces him to affirm, in concluding his analysis on Wicksell's monetary theory:

> what Wicksell is essentially saying is that the level of money prices is indeterminate as long as the quantity of money is not fixed, and that continuous changes in the quantity of money will cause continuous changes in the 'price' (value) of money relative to other commodities. But the same statement can be made for the relative price of potatoes – if the quantity of potatoes in the market is continuously changing. (Patinkin, 1965, p. 596)

Patinkin does not ask himself why the quantity of 'money' may not be fixed and why continuous changes in its quantity may be produced. The innovative part of Wicksell's scheme with regard to the quantity theory of money to which the latter wanted to oppose himself is once again ignored. The obvious consequence of such an attitude is that Patinkin has to equate 'money' with 'potatoes', for only by means of this equalisation is he capable of offering, somehow, an explanation of a crucial aspect of the Wicksellian theory. Indeed, *this* is the thesis that has been advanced throughout the present analysis.

The merit of Patinkin consists in the fact that by means of his own words this particular kind of equalisation is made explicit. This of course relieves the present writer of the embarrassing task of stating that ultimately, according to Patinkin, 'money' and 'potatoes' are the same thing.

NOTES

1. In another reference context, A. Leijonhufvud (1981, p. 160) ascribes the existence and persistence of disequilibrium to the lack of 'coordination' between the decisions of the banks and of the entrepreneurs: the former by pursuing a wrong interest policy, since they do not perceive the 'right' intertemporal preference expressed by the savers and the entrepreneurs (and reflected in the natural rate of interest), the latter because they do not realise the inflationary (or deflationary) consequences the banking policy produces.

    It would seem to be impossible to adopt such a reasoning for interpreting the Wicksellian scheme on the basis of the thesis presented here, for the problem of non-equilibrium cannot trivially be *reduced* to a problem

A Critique of the Orthodox Interpretation

of 'information'. In this connection it is worth recalling that Leijonhufvud refers, for the notion of equilibrium, to that adopted by F. H. Hahn (1973, p. 25), according to which 'an economy is in equilibrium when it generates messages which do not cause agents to change the theories which they hold or the policies which they pursue'.

2. This is said according to the principle of the quantity theory of money.

7 The Itinerary of Hicks

7.1

The interpretation of Wicksell offered by Patinkin, discussed in the previous chapter, can be said to represent the most 'orthodox' neoclassical interpretation found in the literature. It is, however, possible to trace a more 'flexible' version of it, in Hicks.

Wicksell's monetary theory is taken into consideration by Hicks in his three very well-known works covering a span of almost forty years, and the feature of 'flexibility' essentially consists in the fact that starting his interpretation from an orthodox neoclassical viewpoint he passes through a less rigid version of it to end in a *sui generis* interpretation which is, for the main purposes of the present work, the most interesting one.

Hick's itinerary begins from his 1939 book *Value and Capital* (Hicks, 1946, 1st edn 1939). Hicks's reasoning is addressed to the search for the conditions assuring the stability of the temporary equilibrium of the system considered – equilibrium which is referring to a unit period of time. In this connection the ratio between the proportional increase of a commodity's expected price and the proportional increase of the same commodity's current price – a ratio defined by Hicks as 'elasticity of expectations' relative to a determinate agent (1946, p. 205) – plays a crucial role in defining the stability conditions mentioned above. It is interesting to see how they play this crucial role, especially with regard to the Wicksellian scheme.

If the numerical value of the above defined ratio were zero or at most less than unity, this would mean that changes in current prices are considered as *temporary*. Under these circumstances it is then logical to expect a 'temporal substitution' among the various goods by the economic agents.

Taking for example an increase in the price of a good, this will produce an increase in its supply to satisfy the implicit increase in its demand. The working-out of the substitution effect is then the stability mechanism, in the sense that it prevents the disequilibrium state from reproducing itself.

But if the elasticity of price expectation is equal to unity, the opportunity of substitution over time among the various goods does not exist. Now an increase in the price of a good will no longer produce an increase in its supply. In the Wicksellian case of a proportional increase of all the prices, this will induce an equal increase in *expected* prices, and thus an increase in prices paid by entrepreneurs will be exactly balanced by the increase (of equal amount) they will expect in the prices of their products. The demand and the supply position of the various goods will remain unchanged; given their initial equality, it will continue to be so even *after* the increase in prices. An increase in the demand for a good, in money terms, will produce a corresponding increase in price but *not*, at the same time, an increase in its supply; this will result in another increase in price.

In the situation so far depicted, although not a disequilibrium one (since the demand for and the supply of a good are equal), the stability mechanisms are not fully working: the stability of the system is, as Hicks maintains, *imperfect* (1946, p. 248) and this is due to the fact that the elasticity of expectation is equal to unity. It goes without saying that for a numerical value greater than unity the 'stability' of the system would exceed the limits of simple 'imperfection'; it would transform itself into instability: an increase, for example, in all the prices would produce a state in which every demand would be greater than supply. The unit value of the elasticity of expectations constitutes, then, the watershed between stability and instability of the system.

By means of this key reading, the prime responsibility of the Wicksellian cumulative process is imputed to the value which the elasticity of expectations assumes: with *at least* a unit value that process must take place, since the subjects believe that price variation is *permanent*. In contrast to Patinkin, who referred to the behaviour of the banking system in relation to the working of the stability mechanisms, Hicks makes reference to the behaviour of the economic subjects in general – banks excluded. Even when he discusses possible stabilisers (ibid, ch. 21) – rate of interest, contracts, price rigidity – the banking system is always out of the scheme.

Not all of Hicks's reasoning is as convincing. He himself acknowledges this, which will be discussed presently, and this has induced him to modify some of his positions during subsequent years. There are some, however, which deserve to be taken into consideration immediately.

Hicks, as noted, attributes to the elasticity of expectations a determinant role in the development of affairs, particularly in the cumulative process. It appears, however, evident that the state of expectations *in itself* never emerges as the *primum movens* – using Wicksell's expression. Although Hicks himself points it out also, the initial phase of the development of the process always consists in a variation in the money rate of interest relative to the natural rate created by the banking system, *ceteris paribus*. Therefore the process starts from *this* fact. Hicks, however, in the 1939 book, attributes to it a secondary weight and the emphasis is instead on the behaviour of the economic subjects, not in direct relation to the admitted variation, but on the basis of a predetermined hypothesis regarding the type of reaction possessed by any single economic subject. A consequence of such an attitude is that he starts from an assumed variation in prices (which is then not explained) for analysing subsequently, in relation to this, the possible alternative attitudes of the agents upon which the maintenance or not of that variation depends. In this however one can hardly find the cause of that variation, that is the divergence of the money rate from the natural rate of interest. Variations in prices, then, are assumed to be independent variables, instead of their being explained within the scheme of reference. On the other hand, the hypothetical values assumed by the elasticity of price expectations cannot all be put on the same footing. Assuming, for example, a value less than unity, would mean, as has been seen, making the hypothesis of *temporary* variations in prices. But on what is it based? Evidently on psychological subjective factors having no direct relation to the concrete development of business. As soon as one refers to such factors, it is difficult to accept the hypothesis of a value of the elasticity null or less than unity.

This is why such an hypothesis is not to be found in Wicksell. The minimum base from which to start is that, instead, the subjects make their initial calculations with reference to the level of prices attained up to that moment. They then take into account all that is happening in the economic system. It is always on this presupposition that Wicksell introduces the hypothesis of 'elasticity of price expectations' (using the Hicksian term) greater than unity, for it is the *objective experience*, consolidated over a certain span of time of the cumulative process, that *induces* the subjects to change their expectations; which, thus, are not automatically given once and for all and outside the context of reference.

Hicks, in another part of his work, had classified three distinct kinds of influences to which price expectations can be subjected:

One sort is entirely non-economic: the weather, the political news, people's state of health, their 'psychology'. Another is economic, but still not closely connected with actual price-movements; it will include mere market superstitions, at the one extreme, and news bearing on future movements of demand or supply (e.g. crop reports), at the other. The third consists of actual experience of prices, experience in the past and experience in the present; it is this last about which we can find most to say. (1946, p. 204)

But, as has been seen, the influences on expectations making for the hypothesis of a value of the elasticity null or less than unity (for which values the cumulative process could not be possible) do not belong to the last type considered by Hicks in the quoted passage; they belong instead to the first type as if they were 'autonomous' expectations.

Thus, the problem of perfect or imperfect stability and instability breaks down, especially the basic reference to numerical values of the elasticity of price expectations upon which, according to Hicks, the existence and the maintenance of the Wicksellian cumulative process would depend.

Hicks himself, however, realises that the dynamic process he describes, and consisting of a series of temporary equilibrium states developing over time, does contain something wrong in his working-out of it. In *Capital and Growth*, in fact, it is openly declared that in the 1939 dynamic system the link between one period and the next is missing, for everything happens and is determined exclusively *within* the period in which the temporary equilibrium is established. In such a case the process is dynamic only in name, and actually is 'quasi-static' (Hicks, 1965, p. 66).

The reason for that is found in the way in which the 'rules of functioning' of the expectations are stated: the possible adjustment of price expectations takes place within the *same* period in which price variations take place too; in other words, the sequence: (i) current price variations influence price expectations, (ii) the latter influence current price variations, takes place without lags. This cannot be admitted in a dynamic analysis. Following Lindahl's suggestions (1939, part II), the correction consists in introducing a *lag* in the adjustment, whatever be its length. Once it is introduced, the periods making up the sequence will be *linked* together.

In *Capital and Growth*, even after having made this 'correction', the interpretation of the Wicksellian cumulative process does not undergo any substantial modification. The fundamental role of expectations, in such a process, is not only reconfirmed, but in addition it is also emphasised that they have a particular function as adjustment 'mechanisms'. Suppose there is a divergence between the money and the natural rate of interest, by what method can the cumulative process be terminated? Clearly, changes on the side of the production of goods cannot constitute a valid starting-point for their equalisation; but the *time* necessary for technology to produce those effects is in general different from the time employed by expectations in adjusting themselves after changes in current prices have taken place. And so, Hicks's reasoning continues, as long as they are highly sensitive – that is, the period of adjustment is extremely short – 'changes in resources cannot make much difference to the Wicksellian cumulative process' (Hicks, 1965, p. 64). It would be a different matter if, instead, expectations were assumed to change extremely slowly, with quite long periods of adjustment.

7.2

A new solution to interpreting the Wicksellian scheme is offered by Hicks himself a few years later (Hicks, 1977) – new, that is, with respect to what he was saying before, as well as to the general attitude of the economic literature on the subject.

First of all the reference to 'expectations', as a crucial element in the functioning of the cumulative process, is left out. This is not so much because it is not possible to give a logical explanation of the cumulative process in those terms.[1]

It is Hicks himself who admits that a version of that process whose pivot lies on the state of expectations is an overstatement and, from a historical point of view, 'probably an anachronism' (Hicks, 1977, p. 67).

The cumulative process can be illustrated going back to Wicksell, but with a 'variation' explained by Hicks in the following way (ibid, pp. 67–8). Let us suppose, as before, a relative diminution of the money rate of interest. This will produce a different distribution between demand and supply of capital goods on the one hand and of consumption goods on the other; more specifically, a relative increase in demand for the former will take place with respect to a supply temporarily unchanged. Here the Hicksian 'sequence' is becoming 'wider' compared with the analogous Wicksellian one. In fact, the different distribution between demand and supply will produce an increase in prices of some capital goods.

There is *however* an *interval* of time between two different price increases, such that the prices of some goods (supposed input by Hicks) are *already* increased and those of others (output) *not yet* increased. Along the same lines, there will come into being a 'pseudo-natural rate' lower than the natural one and tending to the money rate, so that the system is temporarily brought back to equilibrium. But as soon as the demand for consumption goods increases, the corresponding prices will increase as well, so that the 'pseudo-natural rate' will rise again towards the natural rate proper, and the cumulative process will be repeating itself as usual. The latter version, however, shows some dissonances in comparison with the former, especially with the Wicksellian scheme. Disregarding in fact the way in which the temporal sequence develops, in the last version it is quite hard to understand the coming into scene of the 'pseudo-natural rate'. If one supposes a closed economic system (for example, the world economy as a whole) – the same hypothesis made by Hicks, following Wicksell – the increase in the prices of the 'input' is not one-way; prices greater than before are paid *by* entrepreneurs *to other* entrepreneurs, so that to higher outlets correspond higher receipts. It is therefore difficult to foretell whether the 'rate of money return on investments' decreases, as supposed by Hicks, or not.

However, more important than the internal development of this new Hicksian version of the Wicksell scheme, two characteristic aspects of the Wicksellian approach invite discussion.

The first concerns the distinction between phenomena relative to the 'cycle' and those related to the 'trend'. The *interval* which Hicks speaks about is essentially related to the former, whereas in Wicksell the attention is on medium-term problems.

But the second apsect is the most relevant one. It starts from the consideration that in the face of price movements different from each other, as in the case of a process of accumulation, it becomes extremely difficult to say what sort of price stability defines an equilibrium position (Hicks, 1977, p. 69). This is certainly not a new problem: in discussing the scheme of a monetary economy in Chapter 2 we analysed Sraffa's 'fundamental' objection to the Wicksellian criterion of stabilising the price level, ultimately consisting in the *impossibility* of having, in the supposed case of accumulation, a *unique* price level to stabilise, compatible with a *unique* natural rate of reference for banking policy.

More specifically, let us assume an increase in productivity and thus, *ceteris paribus*, a diminution in the 'cost of labour'. In such a case one can conceive of *an* 'equilibrium' with the prices (of the goods involved in the increasing productivity) relatively decreasing and constant money wages; or, the opposite case, *another* 'equilibrium' with constant prices and increasing money wages; or any of the *infinite* combinations of the above two cases.

> How does one distinguish between these alternatives, or between the obvious compromises which might be constructed between them, so as to dignify one, rather than another, with the title of equilibrium? There does not appear to be any, within the Wicksell model, by which one can distinguish.
>
> It must, however, be insisted that in spite of the ambiguity, thus encountered, the central Wicksell doctrine is unchanged. (Hicks, 1977, pp. 69–70)

This very admission by Hicks is of great importance for the key reading proposed in the present work. His itinerary ends up with a viewpoint completely new with respect to the tradition of thought which 'hibernated' Wicksell in the stereotyped neoclassical world. A set of statements, however, reinforces Hicks's position relative to the problem now under discussion, making it more explicit. In fact, if on the one hand the problem of the choice of the equilibrium, among the many possible, turns out to be 'indeterminate', on the other 'if we are interested in the prime monetary problems, of inflation and deflation, *something else must be introduced, from outside*' (ibid, pp. 70–1; italics added). And in a much clearer way he adds:

> We are to select a particular equilibrium (out of the many Wicksellian equilibria now seen to be possible) and to regard it as *the* equilibrium, which against all others is to be preferred. But we can only do this on *non-monetary considerations*. It can be no more than the course which the economy, in its institutional structure, can most easily follow. Such a course may be one in which prices (as represented by some particular price-index) are constant, or falling, or rising. Monetary considerations alone do not tell us which.

Such an equilibrium, nevertheless, is still an equilibrium, in Wicksell's sense; it can be disturbed by a monetary policy which is inappropriate to it. (Hicks, 1977, p. 71; italics added, save the first one)

7.3

If one of the fundamental features emerging from the Wicksellian scheme is the singling-out of an equilibrium based on considerations of a non-monetary nature, there is however another one to add. It essentially consists, as will be evident in a moment, in the fact that the selected 'equilibrium' only fulfils the role of being the reference point, not the position towards which the system tends to converge. (The first is the minimum required for defining 'equilibrium', and for reasons already stated and analysed does possess the feature of being able to be 'changed' at any time.) This has been pointed out elsewhere (Chapter 6, Section 2), and though Hicks does not make it explicit, this characteristic can be traced, and made perfectly compatible with the given interpretation, by connecting it with another in a different part of Hicks's aforementioned essay.

In Hicks's version of the classical theory of money (1977, pp. 50–61) (that is, the quantity theory of money), he not only proves the existence of an equilibrium path, but also makes clear – as far as it is of interest here – that possible monetary fluctuations take place *around* that equilibrium path, which performs thus the function of a 'gravitation path'. First of all the likelihood of those fluctuations is connected to the 'primitive' credit system existing in a economy where loans are transacted without the intervention of an organised banking system, and thus directly between man and man. A prolonged demand for loans greater than the accumulated monetary funds leads to extinguishing the latter without the possibility of meeting the requests with higher and higher rates of interests – hence a 'roof' to expansion and the subsequent reverse tendency toward equilibrium, due also to the willingness of lenders to rebuild their monetary funds and thus to reduce their expenditures. This process can continue *beyond* equilibrium but *not beyond* a given 'floor', characterised by zero loans but at the same time by an exogenous supply of metallic money, and here Hicks quite reasonably deems it absurd that it will exclusively be channelled into the hands of those who want to 'accumulate'. Under such circumstances there will then exist the minimum conditions for a 'recovery', with new demand for and new supply of funds, again bringing the economy towards equilibrium – in which the excess of saving (positive or negative) is zero and thus the generated income is proportional to the supply of money. The absence of the banking system, therefore, does not exclude the possibility of fluctuations; but the mechanism of the private market loan makes the fluctuations *bounded*, upward and downward with respect to the equilibrium path. This feature could equally well be produced even if the banking system were present, with the condition however that the basic money was uniquely made up of metallic money, with no other types of money, like bank money, fulfilling any role whatsoever. This is in fact the case under the *gold standard*, in its crude form: an increase, for example, in the value of the product above that of equilibrium will result in a drain in the reserves of gold to an 'unsustainable' upper limit; likewise for the lower one. In the same way, one cannot say the system remains rigidly constrained around an equilibrium trend, but its fluctuations are *bounded* around it.

In both cases the fundamental feature is an *exogenous* quantity of money. It should not be surprising therefore that with or without a banking system Hicks makes no distinction in the way in which monetary fluctuations take place. When the banking system is present, the limits to these fluctuations are traced by the *bounded* policy performed by the banking system itself, for it is constrained by a management of a quantity of money *given from outside*. This is perfectly similar to the Patinkin banking system, analysed previously. However, Hicks remarks, as soon as one attributes to the banking system a power in the management of bank money, thus *not* given from outside – as from a historical point of view – the supply of money is not the exogenous variable any more, but monetary policy is (cf. Hicks, 1977, p. 61).[2]

This can be clearly seen in the Wicksellian scheme, not only in the pure credit case, but also in the more realistic case of a 'blend' between pure credit and pure cash. Under the latter circumstances the possible introduction of a banking management detached from gold, to put it briefly, is a sufficient element to break the limits, upper and lower, found under the hypothesis of an exogenous money supply. It is precisely what happens in the Wicksell scheme, where the selected equilibrium path can never be a 'gravitation path'.

This extension of Hicks's interpretation seems to mark a departure from a tradition of thought repeatedly referred to. Moreover, if the

The Itinerary of Hicks

arguments contained in the last section constitute the final outline of Hicks's itinerary, they can also be used as a basis for opening a new analysis, especially an inquiry on the relationship between Wicksell and the so-called Swedish School. The following chapter will offer some suggestions for an analysis, without however recalling similar topics already discussed at large in the literature.[3]

NOTES

1. As Hicks restates (1977, pp. 66–7), following for a moment the lines of reasoning contained in his previous works, by starting from an equilibrium position and making the hypothesis of a reduction in the money rate of interest with respect to the natural rate, bank loans expand and prices begin to rise at first; if however the increment of the latter is thought by the entrepreneurs to be *temporary*, this will interrupt the process of loan expansion and prices increase, for expectations are for prices lower than before. What now occurs *because* of that expectation is a natural rate lower than that at the start, denoted by Hicks as a 'pseudo-natural rate' which at first will coincide with the money rate. What has happened is simply the termination of the dynamic process of expansion of the bank loans and of the increase in prices and a return to the initial conditions.

   If the money rate is again lower than the natural rate the process will be repeated. However, if this happens *repeatedly* over time, there exists a moment in which price expectations become anchored to the higher level they have reached. In this way a 'pseudo-natural rate' will no longer occur, or, if one prefers, it will not be identical to the natural rate proper, which being by hypothesis higher than the money rate will constitute the condition for the maintenance of the cumulative process.
2. One should note that in this case reference is made to an exogenous monetary *policy* – different from Ricardo's monetary framework in which the instability more restrictively derives from an exogenous money *supply*.
3. As well as the two essays of B. Ohlin (1937a; 1937b), see C. G. Uhr (1951), E. F. Heckscher (1953), T. Palander (1953), A. Lerner (1953), D. Hammarskjöld (1955), K. G. Landgren (1957), R. Dehem (1957), B. Ohlin (1960), D. Winch (1966), G. L. S. Shackle (1967, chs 9, 10), B. Gustafsson (1973), O. Steiger (1976; 1978), B. Ohlin (1977; 1978), D. Patinkin (1978), W. P. Yohe (1978), C. Hamilton (1979).

8 The Swedish School

Lindahl, Myrdal and Ohlin are usually known in the literature as the most outstanding economists of the so-called Swedish School of the first generation after Wicksell's death. If, however, by the denomination of Swedish School one means a strand of thought almost homogeneous and compact, having in common some cultural roots, it is crucially important to note the *reference* assumed. Compared with Keynes, for example, there is no doubt that the above-mentioned economists do constitute a group or a 'school', often viewed as alternative and generally in opposition to him. But compared with Wicksell, it does not seem legitimate, strangely and paradoxically enough, to treat the Swedish School in terms referred to above. Lindahl and Ohlin, in fact, far beyond their own *formal* declarations have substantially given a content and a development to their contributions which seem quite different from the Wicksellian 'base' from which they start. Moreover their respective works are profoundly different from each other, not only in approach but also in their interpretation of Wicksell. In what follows, then, an attempt will be made to give evidence to such statements.

What has been said in the last part of the discussion on Hicks's itinerary (regarding the features of 'equilibrium' in the Wicksellian scheme) will be the reference base for the discussion of the authors referred to above. Parallel to this will run the other discussion concerning the different ways and intentions of the critiques made by each one of the Wicksellian theoretical schemes.

8.1

In an essay which appeared in 1929 but was published in 1930, Lindahl (1939)[1] formulates several alternative models (ibid, part II, chs 1, 2, 3) in which the effects of a monetary policy expressed by means of hypothetical interest rate variations are analysed relative to the price level. The methods used for that purpose are those of the temporary equilibrium, by means of which the formation of prices is expressed through a system of equations which is valid in *each* period considered and related to equilibrium states, in terms of demand and supply, of the period itself. In this way price variations and price level will both depend upon variations of all the factors determining those prices and which are assumed to take place at the moment of transition from one period to the next.

The hypotheses which are at the basis of such models follow the commonest hypotheses already met in the Wicksellian scheme, namely a closed economy, an autonomous monetary policy, a centralised credit, a pure credit system. The development of the affairs, however, taking place in the economic system considered, and on the basis of the different 'complications' gradually introduced, is quite different from what happens in the Wicksellian scheme. First of all, monetary policy is able to perform an 'active' role *uniquely* in the case in which the economic agents of the system are in a state of complete uncertainty and imperfect foresight. Thus this implies a concrete development of the affairs generally different from what the individuals were expecting. This implies, in turn, the formation of different expectations for every individual in the face of the same events as well as different degrees of reaction. In the opposite case, that is in a world of 'perfect' foresight, the development of prices will exclusively depend on the anticipations made by any single individual and the policy fulfilled by the monetary authority will turn out to be 'passive', in the sense of following an interest rate policy in line with *those* predictions, in order *not to disturb* the equilibrium.

In the first case, more realistically, one makes the hypothesis of starting from a stationary state disturbed by a sudden decrease in the rate of interest on loans performed by the banks. The immediate effect of this, according to Lindahl's reasoning, is an alteration in the profitability of various kinds of investment, in favour of those productions requiring relatively 'longer' periods. Now, according to the various alternative hypotheses introduced (full employment or not, rigid or flexible investment period) there will correspondingly be different developments of the relevant economic variables of the system considered. But it is necessary here to particularly point out some results decidedly different from those which could be obtained from an analogous Wicksellian scheme, as well as the reason for this. The first is the absolute uselessness, within Lindahl's scheme, of any notion of 'natural' rate of interest:

> Whatever rate of interest is established for loans in such a community, wages and other factor prices will be *adapted* to this rate, with the result that stationary conditions can be maintained, if we disregard the fact that unforeseen changes may under certain

conditions destroy the equilibrium. The absolute height of the loan rate of interest is thus of great importance as determining the distribution of output between capitalists and factor owners. But it *does not necessarily exercise any influence* upon movements of the general price level. (Lindahl, 1939, p. 167; italics added)

The case here selected, analysed by Lindahl, seems to clearly point out, through the conclusion already quoted, that a supposed variation in the rate of interest on loans, although producing a series of changes in the relevant magnitudes of the system, brings the economy to a *new equilibrium* position. The passage from one position to another is then uniquely a transition in which – as Lindahl shows – a variation in money prices does not necessarily take place.

The parting from Wicksell's point of view, therefore, is quite remarkable. In Lindahl, in fact, the 'intermediate stage', on which Wicksell was particularly insistent, does not exist, or rather it exists simply as a phase of 'redefinition of data' of the system as a consequence of a change in one of them, and the mechanisms bringing the system from one position to another are all of a strictly economic kind.

The process put in motion by a diminution of the rate of interest on loans meets, then, a definite limit: 'when the supply of capital has been increased until it corresponds to the new rate of interest' (Lindahl, 1939, p.181) – a conclusion not at all new, but perfectly in line with the rules of traditional economic theory.

Lindahl himself clarifies the reasons for his rebuttal of the Wicksellian notion of 'normal' rate of interest, whose feature is that of corresponding to the 'natural' rate. He states that only in special cases can one speak of a natural rate as 'independent from the price system'. Such a case comes into being, for example, in the Ricardian corn/corn model (ibid, p. 267). With more realistic assumptions, and outside this model, the comparison between the invested input and the corresponding output cannot be made by exclusively referring to purely technological conditions, for one has to refer to the price system also, and the 'real' rate of interest 'cannot be regarded as existing independently of the loan rate of interest' (ibid, p. 248).

As to the first part of that critique, Lindahl seems however to bark up the wrong tree, relating to Wicksell. In fact, from a true proposition – the 'real' rate of interest cannot be calculated without referring to prices, in a system in which the employed means of production are heterogeneous – he draws the wrong conclusion: that is, that in the latter case one cannot speak of a 'natural' rate of interest.[2]

As to the second part of that critique, Lindahl also includes in the 'price relations' the current rate of interest on loans:

> The real interest factor in a certain period can be expressed as the relation between anticipated future product value (with appropriate reductions for risk) and the value invested during the period. The prices of invested services are, however, influenced by the demand of entrepreneurs, and these in turn are influenced by the loan rate of interest itself. When this rate is *low*, the demand for services to be invested in the production of real capital rises, and their price therefore *rises to the point* where the invested value may be supposed to bear interest at the current loan rate. (Lindahl, 1939, p. 248; italics added)

It is certain and obvious that the current rate of interest does enter the development of economic affairs. But Lindahl makes it enter in a very particular *way*, compared with how Wicksell does: *whatever be* its new value (compared with before), necessary changes will take place in the economy to reestablish, in general, the initial equilibrium position. In this sense, believing in a 'natural' rate of interest as distinct from the 'money' rate is useless. A value of the rate of interest on loans different from the previous one represents, in the scheme now under discussion and in contrast to Wicksell, a 'breakdown' of the equilibrium, and the consequent dynamic process which follows from that acts only temporarily to bring the system *from* a state of equilibrium *to* another – like the similar process taking place in the Patinkin scheme, previously analysed.

Some of the statements found in the passage quoted above must, then, be interpreted in a different way from that in which one would be tempted to do following the Wicksellian line: a 'low' rate of interest on loans, in Wicksell's terms, would be meaningless, whereas in Lindahl's it would not be, for it is not the difference between that rate and the natural rate which matters, but exclusively the fact that the former is *different* (in this case, lower) from that previously fixed. What happens in the transition does not matter, being simply a normal 'adjustment'. In this connection, it is no surprise that

> the real rate of interest on capital, as here defined, has a *tendency to adjust itself* to the actual loan rate of interest *in every period*.

Agreement between the real rate and the loan rate in a certain period, therefore provides no foundation for characterizing the latter as 'normal'. (Lindahl, 1939, p. 249; italics added)

Since in period after period the equilibrium position becomes reestablished, it is trivial to speak of a 'normal' rate of interest in Lindahl's scheme, for basically this rate is ultimately *always* an *equilibrium* rate; on the other hand, 'normality' would be meaningful if compared with 'abnormality', which being non-existent makes the former non-existent too.

It is also interesting to note that between Wicksell and Lindahl there exist some 'asymmetries of movement'. In Wicksell, in fact, a rate of interest on loans is supposed given, in the face of a supposed change in the conditions of profitability. The process which is then put in motion does not terminate until a banking policy for the interest rate fails to move in the direction indicated by the new conditions of profitability; but for what has been said that policy does not start to operate. In contrast, in Lindahl the conditions of profitability are supposed given, and the *primum movens* is assumed to take place through a change in the current rate of interest on loans. The analogous process which is put in motion, to which reference has been made repeatedly above, takes place through changes in the conditions of profitability, and this happens according to well-known market mechanisms.

In the first case, then, the adjustment to the new equilibrium position does *not* take place automatically, for this depends on a *banking policy* decision, which *may* be taken 'immediately', or 'late' or 'never'. But in the second case the adjustment to equilibrium takes place *always*, for this depends on the ever-present and working market mechanisms.

Under the conditions so postulated by Lindahl it becomes obvious that *any* development of the price level be compatible with that of the 'dynamic process'. What effectively matters is only the attainment of a new equilibrium position, and for this any *level* of price suffices. From this originates the explicit rebuttal by Lindahl of the terms 'inflation' and 'deflation' (1939, pp. 255–6, fn.).

In spite, then, of some 'radicalism', the contribution so far discussed seems to have almost vanished or brought Wicksell's contributions back to the traditional rules of economic theory. This first step by an eminent economist of the Swedish School was not regarded negatively in England (one has to remember that Lindahl's book was published in England in 1939, though Lindahl had been working on a translation with Ursula Webb – later Mrs Hicks – since 1935), where the Keynesian theory wished openly to represent itself as an alternative to the dominant economic theory. In the same year (1939) Myrdal's contribution, *Monetary Equilibrium*, was also published.

8.2

In contrast to Lindahl, who makes a critique of Wicksell's monetary theory by constructing alternative schema of reference, Myrdal instead subjects the whole Wicksellian approach to an 'immanent criticism' (Myrdal, 1939, pp. 30–1) which essentially consists in a redefinition of the various conditions singling out a 'monetary equilibrium'. The use of this notion, which was rejected by Lindahl – as has been seen above – is one of the most characteristic aspects of Myrdal's work (ibid, p. 31, fn. 2, in which Myrdal summarises his critique of Lindahl's work). The latter underlines, however, the instrumental character of that notion, and in particular that the conditions defining monetary equilibrium should certainly not require the expressing of 'virtual reality or tendency' of the economic system for their attainment (ibid, p. 40). He starts, then, from the three conditions defining Wicksell's monetary equilibrium:

(1) equality between the natural rate and the money rate of interest
(2) equality between savings and 'investments'
(3) a constant level of price.

Each of these conditions is subjected to a concise criticism by Myrdal, especially the third one, as will be seen presently; but the principal pivot around which his argumentations revolve consists in the following. Once 'money' is introduced into the economic system *each* variable and any relation contained in it *cannot* be autonomously determined or specified – i.e., without referring to monetary variables and the connected phenomena derived from them. This is a very ambitious project, and is actually *the* project of monetary theory which Myrdal attempts through his immanent criticism of the Wicksellian theory. So, for example, he rejects the notion of a 'natural rate of interest' as distinct and autonomous with respect to the money rate; and, through the same logic, he rejects the idea of assuming as 'constant and given' the relative prices of commodities once monetary phenomena are introduced into the scheme. The latter do not simply *influence* the relative prices (or 'price relations' in Myrdal's terminology) but redefine the characteristics of them:

> The accounting unit receives, through credit contracts, a real importance for the exchange relations; for the process of price formation is then influenced by *changes* in the exchange value of the monetary unit with respect to other commodities . . . the conditions on which credit is given and taken – here quite abstractly represented by 'money rates of interest' – themselves influence these relative prices and through the relative prices the exchange value productivity of real capital.[3] Our conclusion, therefore, must be that credit and money rate of interest must be included even in the formula by which the natural rate of interest is defined. (Myrdal, 1939, pp. 52–3)

This being the case, it is consequential for Myrdal not to accept the Wicksellian picture – contained in *Interest and Prices* (cf. Wicksell, 1898b, ch. 8)[4] – of money as a 'cloak' which can *logically* be put over a procedure of barter exchanges. The latter, according to Myrdal, could only be imagined by assuming perfectly stationary conditions, which in implying constant relative prices make the variations in the value of money take place uniformly for all the commodities. But in non-stationary conditions in the face of variations in the value of money there are changed relative prices 'and credit has therefore at each interest rate a different significance for the profitability of different kinds of entrepreneurs' activity and consequently for the exchange relations' (Myrdal, 1939, p. 52, fn. 2).

8.3

Parallel to the critique now briefly illustrated, a very strong attack is contained in Myrdal's work here under discussion against the third condition for Wicksell's monetary equilibrium, that is against a constant price level. After having shown that in order to depict a monetary equilibrium it is necessary and sufficient that a set of 'price relations' is attained for which the equality between savings and investments ex-ante exists, he shows that such a condition turns out to be compatible with *any* development of money prices, for the

The Swedish School

latter do not perform any role in defining the formula expressing the above equality (Myrdal, 1939, p. 132). For this 'theorem' to be fully operational, the hypothesis of perfectly flexible prices is necessary. This, however, cannot be admitted in a 'realistic' scheme. Here, in fact, one has first to make the hypothesis of credit contracts having fixed rates of interest and other kinds of contracts of relatively long duration; second, 'a general element of inertia' (ibid, p. 134) should be admitted, which characterises some prices in their movement, such that their reaction to adjustment can be relatively speedier or slower; this, in particular, is evidently put forward in the case of prices subject to monopolistic or administrative conditions. In any case the feature of 'stickiness' of some prices makes a constraint on the general movement of prices, such that correspondingly a monetary policy directed to the maintaining of monetary equilibrium must adapt the more flexible prices to those less flexible, in the sense that the general price level has to follow a movement allowing for the least possible change of the 'sticky' prices in order not to disturb the price equilibrium relations (ibid, pp. 133–7).

The conclusion of the reasoning, thus, is that no general movement of prices can be taken as a reference for monetary equilibrium.

To this 'indeterminateness' another is paralleled. The single 'money rate of interest' – which has followed the various argumentations so far made – that one assumes to represent heterogeneous credit conditions, makes it possible to conceive *different combinations* of money interest rates which in any given situation produce the same effect in bringing about a monetary equilibrium (ibid, p. 159). An 'indifference field' (or 'indeterminateness') of monetary equilibrium is thus created, within which determinate variations in credit conditions are possible, one in comparison with the other, without this upsetting the general condition for the existence and maintenance of monetary equilibrium.

In the definition of the 'indifference field', the factors outside it, both of an economic and non-economic nature, are supposed to be given one at a time, but in so far as they change (and on condition that there is no compensating by the variation of other factors) they determine a simultaneous variation in the 'indifference field' itself, in the sense of either shrinking it or widening it (ibid, pp. 159–60).

Granted all that, it follows that a monetary equilibrium can be fundamentally attained through two routes: the first by means of different combinations of 'credit conditions':

> these different combinations are not politically indifferent but necessarily signify a discrimination between various types of demand for credit. Now, as the existing conditions in society make different kinds of credit demands of varying importance to the different branches of the economy, and also, within these branches, to the large and small entrepreneurs, the more and the less capitalistic, and the members of all the other categories, therefore, various social groups would be interested in the different combinations of credit conditions. In other words, they would be interested in different regulations of the individual parts of the complex, 'rate of interest', by means of which profit margins, appropriate to the balance in the capital market, are maintained. (Myrdal, 1939, p. 182)

This means, for example, that 'two credit situations of differing degrees of "easiness" in both of which the monetary equilibrium relations are in balance, would have different effects, particularly upon the distribution of income and wealth' (ibid, p. 183).

The second route goes through the set of those factors, distinct from those strictly of a monetary nature and supposed initially given, which contribute to the configuration of monetary equilibrium, in particular in the determination of the dimension of the 'indifference field'. In such a sense, the maintenance of a monetary equilibrium

> becomes a question not only of monetary policy but of economic policy as a whole, social policy and the institutions which rule the labour market, cartel legislation and all related factors. (Myrdal, 1939, p. 184)

It is thus the more general combination of these factors, together with the others relating to the credit conditions, which can produce a monetary equilibrium. For this reason, Myrdal points out, monetary policy cannot be considered from an objective and technical point of view until one wants to pursue a general goal like monetary stabilisation or the elimination of the trade cycle, for the goal can be attained through a multiplicity of routes 'in which all sorts of social and economic problems are given different solutions, and in which the credit screw must be applied more or less severely' (ibid). These elements belongs to that set of factors which are certainly not given data of the problem but, rather, about them turns the political struggle in every country. Scientific discussion must, therefore, make allowance for those political elements in the problem, even if only in the form of alternative hypotheses . . .

The problem of monetary policy cannot possibly be isolated, because a different arrangement of all these factors must give rise to a different monetary policy even under a given general norm; or, in other words, these must invest a given norm with a different real content. Different social groups have thus quite different interests respecting the *method and content* of a monetary policy, aimed at business stability, even if one assumes that this can itself be regarded as an aim common to all. (Myrdal, 1939, pp. 184–5)

Myrdal's point is thus very important to monetary analysis: it consists in the attempt at introducing in a systematic way 'power relations' in the dynamics of the 'economic' variables. His work therefore, can be substantially considered as an important development of Wicksell's theory. However it was published in English in 1939,[5] the same year in which Lindahl's essays appeared in an English edition. In those years the theoretical debates were centred on the 'new' Keynesian theory, published only three years before; and Wicksell, having been an inspiring source for some central parts of Keynes's *Treatise on Money* (Keynes, 1930, vol. I, chs 10, 11, 12),[6] now appeared on the same footing as the *General Theory*, as a 'classic' – according to the new jargon – so that Myrdal's contribution did not receive the attention which it certainly deserved.

But in order to complete this outline, another Swedish contribution should be mentioned, that of Ohlin: not so much by referring to the well-known essays published in the 1937 *Economic Journal*, but to the lesser-known essay, the 'Introduction' to the English translation of *Interest and Prices* published – not unintentionally – in 1936 and – again, not unintentionally – translated by Richard Kahn.[7]

8.4

Out of the fifteen pages of the 'Introduction' Ohlin devotes barely two of them to the historical-cultural context in which that work was conceived and executed and the cultural roots from which it seems to have originated. But from the second page onwards till the end the

'Introduction' is composed of a long list of 'changes' to which the main ideas of *Interest and Prices* would have been subjected, especially by Wicksell himself. Any reader would be justified in concluding that the whole structure of *Interest and Prices* is after all built entirely on air; moreover, according to Ohlin, since those changes do not constitute any 'new' theory, nor any crucial indication for emendation or improvement, one is consequentially induced to believe that it is the very Wicksellian theoretical construction that is unsuitable as a useful reference base in the field of monetary theory.

The justification for an English translation thirty-eight years after the original edition is very hard to understand, on reading Ohlin's 'Introduction'. However, after an analysis of the latter, as will be attempted presently, some further reflection can help in searching for that justification, if one goes back to the cultural-academic climate of theoretical economics in the 1930s.

After having premised that Wicksell regarded his theory as 'an amplification of the old quantity theory' and 'he always regarded his own contribution as a doubtful hypothesis' (Ohlin, 1936, p. viii), Ohlin begins from the 'logical' list of changes referred to above by recalling the long controversy between Wicksell and Davidson[8] which would have led to a 'reconsideration and revision' of what Ohlin defines 'the curious concept of the natural rate of interest' (ibid, p. xii).

In this long controversy, never definitely settled, Wicksell's engaging in a reconsideration of certain aspects of his own monetary theory can be considered a rare occasion. Although that discussion has been the most important one with his contemporaries relative to the monetary theory here considered, it was however not the only one; Wicksell himself in *Lectures II* summarises some objections to his theory (1906, pp. 198–200). The general weight given to them was anyhow considered extremely relative and such as to surely relegate them to 'secondary factors of the problems' (ibid, p. 200).

Such circumstances are also recalled by Ohlin in his 'Introduction' to *Interest and Prices*. At the same time, however, he adds:

> Wicksell was again questioning the whole structure of monetary theory; this was not, however, due to the criticism which he had received but to his own doubts. (Ohlin, 1936, p. xii)

This constitutes the central statement around which the main theme of Ohlin's 'Introduction' revolves. Let us then see what some of these 'doubts' would consist of.

One of them would properly consist in a modification introduced by Wicksell in *Lectures II* with respect to *Interest and Prices* and relative to the concept of natural rate of interest which is substituted by normal rate. On this a clarification has been given previously and it has been argued that behind the new terminology there was hidden the more substantial need of changing the barter scheme into that of credit between man and man.[9]

Another modification introduced by Wicksell would be connected with the influence of gold production on prices. Here Ohlin emphasises the supposed changes, alternately back and forth, which Wicksell would have had in mind without in any way defining his own position once and for all with respect to that problem (Ohlin, 1936, pp. xv–xvi).

With this, in any case, we are still far away from a complete rebuttal by Wicksell of his *Interest and Prices*, in spite of the critiques and doubts which had attacked his main contribution in the field of monetary theory. At this point Ohlin pursues still further his own project:

> During his last years Wicksell came more and more to doubt the solidity of what had been regarded as the cornerstone of his monetary theory: – the idea that if the money rate coincided with a normal rate of interest, which brought about equality between savings and investment, the commodity price level would remain constant. (1936, p. xix)

In order to prove this statement Ohlin explicitly refers to Wicksell's last work, published one year before his death (Wicksell, 1925), and it is important to analyse, though briefly, the basic reasoning contained in this last work in order to verify whether Ohlin's deductions do correspond to his own statement quoted above.

8.5

Wicksell focuses his attention, in the writing now under discussion, on the problem of disentangling causes from effects of inflationary phenomena which had characterised the whole period during and after the First World War.

In the search for the causes of those phenomena two distinct groups had arisen: one embracing the business men, the other the theoretical economists. The former substantially maintained that the scarcity of commodities (in the case of inflation), or the relative abundance of the latter (in the case of deflation), would have been, respectively, the main causes of those phenomena; as a consequence, the expansion, and subsequently the contraction, of the circulating medium was the naturally expected result. Inflation and deflation, therefore, did not find their origin in the 'monetary' sphere but in the 'real' one.

In contrast, the economists – represented in this case by Cassel (1922) – maintained that a decreased supply of commodities should be necessarily joined to a decreased quantity of the money in circulation in order that money prices remain constant. If this does not happen, increases or diminutions of prices must be attributed to an excessively easy monetary policy. It is therefore in the monetary sphere one finds the primary cause of inflationary and deflationary phenomena.

This framework is completely different from that considered within Wicksell's basic theoretical scheme, analysed in the previous pages – and Wicksell himself, as will be shown presently, had drawn attention to this on many occasions. Actually, inflation and deflation of the kind referred to above are related to a *particular* situation, which is that of a war and post-war state; and this is obviously reflected in a *particular* productive structure characterised by a relative diminution of labour employed for civil production and thus, at the same time, by a relative increase in the labour employed for war production. From a strictly economic standpoint the productive processes do *not* now follow a 'normal' course.

Under such circumstances Cassel depicts a triangular framework: in the face of a scarcity of commodities and services on the market households try to keep their own standard of consumption by drawing from their bank deposits. If this happens, banks are bound to reduce credit to firms, and this is directly equivalent to a reduction of their purchasing power and indirectly of that of the families. In this case the goal of keeping constant the standard of consumption fails. But *if* the banks started issuing *new* 'money', as much as was necessary to compensate for the diminution of deposit made by the families, then the purchasing power could be maintained although at a cost of an increase in prices. Hence the conclusion according to which too 'liberal' a credit policy is ultimately responsible for the 'cause' of inflation (Cassel 1922, p. 55).

This approach enabled Wicksell to object that the 'purchasing power' involved in the above reasoning be a simple 'monetary' purchasing power, not an 'effective' one. If prices increase, this will be sufficient to stimulate the creation of an amount of circulating medium *exactly* necessary for the development of business. That is immediately clear if one supposes that such a development takes place through the 'giro' account utilised in the pure credit system by Wicksell: higher prices will *automatically* require registrations for higher amounts. On the other hand, if more realistically the system uses a circulating medium, then the behaviour of the banking system in the situation so far described will turn out to be almost *indifferent* with respect to the phenomenon of price increase. In fact, if the banks do *not* increase the issue of notes, this will at most produce a hindrance in the development of business, for one would make automatic recourse to a corresponding increase in the 'velocity of circulation' of money to meet higher prices. If instead the banks *do* increase the issue of notes, this will simply make the circulating medium adequate for the attained price level. In both cases, therefore, the money purchasing power will adapt itself to a variation in prices whose cause – that is, the scarcity of goods and services – could never be eliminated by it. In both cases, moreover, Cassell's theoretical basis, the quantity theory of money, falls down. In the first case, with a 'passive' monetary policy, the supposed constancy in the velocity of circulation of money is missing, for – as Wicksell underlines – the conservative nature of consumption habits is much stronger than that of payment habits, 'and if the two come into conflict, it should be fairly obvious which will get the upper hand' (Wicksell, 1925, p. 202).

In the second case, with an 'accommodating' monetary policy, the purchasing power, in money terms, which follows from it cannot anyway 'be sufficient to procure the quantity of goods which each individual would like to consume; for if it were, everybody, taken together, would obtain more goods than the amount actually on the market, and that is an absurdity' (ibid, p. 201).

The interesting aspect to point out here, related to Ohlin's critique, concerns the interest rate policy of the banks under the particular circumstance created by the war state. Such a case, Wicksell remarks, 'leads us to an entirely different *presentation* of the problem from the one on which monetary theory has hitherto been based' (1925, p. 203; italics added). The reason for that is found in Wicksell's *changed framework*:

> Under normal conditions, when production and consumption proceed in almost unchanged proportions, a rise in prices (apart from a rise due to an abnormal increase in the production of gold) can actually be caused only by too liberal a credit policy on the part of the banks, making it possible for speculators to obtain an increase in money purchasing power which no longer corresponds to such increase as may be simultaneously brought about by voluntary saving. (Wicksell, 1925, p. 203; italics added)

But in different conditions, and precisely in a war state in which the 'proportions' between production and consumption are heavily altered and characterised by a natural scarcity of indispensable consumption goods, the interest rate policy adopted by the banks loses almost completely its effectiveness, for now the interested economic subjects, towards whom that restrictive credit policy is directed, are mainly the *consumers*, and no longer the *producers*; and the former will try *in any case* to strengthen their own liquidity position in order to keep unchanged the standard of living so greatly disturbed by the supervening scarcity of commodities on the market, to which no additional creation of purchasing power can offer a remedy. In these circumstances a credit restriction, operated through an increase in the rate of interest, will be without any substantial consequence for inflation, which

> cannot cease until a balance has been attained between the supply and the demand of goods, and this *never* takes place so long as there is a general endeavour to maintain a degree of consumption which it is physically impossible to meet. (Wicksell, 1925, p. 205)

It is only when people submit to a lower standard of living compared with the normal one (since they become accustomed to the permanent scarcity of goods) that 'demand and supply will again correspond to each other on a lower plane, and there will be no cause for a further rise in prices' (ibid); and this will take place with or without credit restriction of the banks.

The hypotheses embodied in this scheme of reference bring, then, different conclusions from those obtained under *other* hypotheses. As regards Wicksell, two distinct interpretative frameworks are involved: *Interest and Prices* and *Lectures II* on the one hand, and on the other, the writing here under discussion. But Ohlin, by ignoring the different framework Wicksell refers to, is led to extract only the *apparent* antithetic results following from that:

> The question of the reaction of the monetary mechanism – in his 1925 paper – is placed in the background and the movement of prices is discussed in terms of total incomes and the total supply commodities. It thus becomes evident that, as in the case discussed by Wicksell, a general rise in prices may well come about because consumers increase their demand, in terms of money, for consumption goods. (Ohlin, 1936, p. xx)

The conclusion one might draw from this, according to Ohlin, would be, 'although it is not formulated by Wicksell' (ibid, p. xxi), that 'even if there is equilibrium between savings and investment, as commonly understood, incomes and prices may rise or fall *ad libitum*' (ibid).

According to such an interpretation, then, 'one of the very fundamentals of Wicksell's original theory would have to be given up' (ibid).

This line of interpretation, however, cannot be accepted. Apart from the reasons so far given, Wicksell himself underlines that his original theoretical scheme must be considered as *distinct* from that in the 1925 essay. In the footnote contained in the latter essay, in replying to some critiques formulated by Cassel and Schumpeter – according to which (in the Schumpeterian version) an interest rate maintained at a high level although it leads initially to a diminution of prices must ultimately lose all its effects, for it tends to diminish production and thus to increase the scarcity of commodities – Wicksell writes:

> For my own part, I have assumed that the volume of production – leaving out those phenomena which are caused by a crisis – will, on the whole, remain *constant* as long as the real factors of production, land, labour, and real capital, remain unaltered. Bank rate affects only the competition between producers for the possession of these factors, causing their prices, and other prices, steadily to sink, or to rise, as long as an abnormally high or low bank rate is in force. If Cassel's view, and still more that of Schumpeter, were

correct, it would be possible for the banks to raise or lower their rates *ad libitum* without risking anything more than a once-and-for-all rise or fall in prices. This seems absurd. (Wicksell, 1925, p. 212)

The thesis is thus restated by Wicksell himself, in opposition to Ohlin's *two distinct* theoretical schema. Ohlin's confusion thus consists in drawing the 'wrong' conclusion from a 'right' reference scheme, or vice versa. As has been noted more than once in this discussion, the inquiry contained in the Wicksellian monetary theory 'is concerned exclusively with such properties of an economic system as do not depend on changes in the scale of production or in the proportions of "factors" (Sraffa, 1960, p. v), a classical hypothesis which Ohlin completely overlooked.

But the 'final' part of Ohlin's 'Introduction' cannot, indeed should not, be avoided. If Wicksell had lived longer and had written other essays, Ohlin would have perhaps found 'further changes' in these too.

According to Ohlin, Wicksell himself would have entrusted others with such a task. In fact, Ohlin concludes by quoting from Wicksell:

As to the period *after* the War, with its irrational and often puzzling price fluctuations, I am loth to confess that I would far sooner listen to somebody who could express an authoritative opinion on these matters than essay an explanation myself. (Wicksell, 1925, p. 210)

Ohlin does not, however, attempt any specification: he does not say that the Wicksellian statement above is simply taken from the text which *opens* the third part of his 1925 essay; he does not say that Wicksell is still talking of the problem of the scarcity of commodities and the connected phenomena of variations of prices in the post-war period, and *not* of 'monetary theory' in general.

But by now we are in 1936, soon after the publication of the 1930 *Treatise on Money* and in the year of the *General Theory*: Wicksell could at last be put on the shelf.

NOTES

1. On the chronology of the publication of the essays included in this work, see in particular the Preface, pp. 15–18.
2. Cf. the discussion made in Chapter 4, section 8. See in particular P. Sraffa (1932, p. 51).
3. With this definition Myrdal replaces Wicksell's 'natural rate of interest'.
4. In *Lectures II*, however, the comparison between a barter economy/monetary economy is replaced by economy with/economy without a banking system. Cf. Chapter 2, section 7.
5. The first version is dated 1931. Cf. G. Myrdal (1939, pp. v–vi).
6. The explicit acknowledgement by Keynes is on p. 167.
7. Apart from the 1907 article (Wicksell, 1907a), the Anglo-Saxon world has practically ignored Wicksell's monetary theory for more than thirty years since its formulation. It is thus surprising that F. W. Taussig (1914), in rejecting for publication in the *Quarterly Journal of Economics* an article by Wicksell (which appears later in a reduced form as a final note in *Lectures II*), admits in a letter dated 7 January 1914 that the works of the Swedish economist, including the 1898 book, 'are not unknown to us'.

   From another point of view, one has to say that Wicksell was never 'warmly' accepted by the Anglo-Saxon academic world. Apart from the 'welcome' reserved by Keynes (with whom Wicksell was able to continue a conversation begun at lunch only by going with the latter to a barber's shop: see T. Gårdlund (1958, p. 295), who quoted extensively from a letter of Wicksell's; and the excuses of J. M. Keynes (1916) in a letter of his dated 26 June 1916 one has to mention another episode as well.

   Wicksell in a letter to E. R. Seligman dated 22 September 1910 (Wicksell, 1910) expressed his willingness to visit the United States and give some seminars at universities. Seligman (1910), in his reply dated 14 October 1910, conveyed to him that all were full up with courses given by foreigners 'for the next year or two'. Wicksell never went to the United States. This episode is not recorded in the biography by T. Gårdlund (1958).
8. A detailed summary of such a controversy can be found in C. G. Uhr (1960, pp. 270–305). Cf. also B. Thomas (1935, pp. 37–40), and B. Thomas (1936, pp. 62–6) where a general valuation of Davidson's economic contributions can be found also. Other writings on this author are E. F. Heckscher (1952) and more recently C. G. Uhr (1975). The sources of the controversy between Wicksell and Davidson are listed in B. Thomas (1936, p. xvi, fn. 5).
9. See note 4 above.

Bibliography

ADARKAR, B. P. (1935) *The Theory of Monetary Policy*, P. S. King & Son, Ltd, London.
ÅKERMAN, J. (1933) 'Knut Wicksell, a Pioneer of Econometrics', *Econometrica*, vol. 1, pp. 113–18.
BAILEY, R. E. (1976) 'On the Analytical Foundations of Wicksell's Cumulative Process', *The Manchester School of Economic and Social Studies*, March, pp. 52–71.
BHADURI, A. (1966) 'The Concept of the Marginal Productivity of Capital and the Wicksell Effect', *Oxford Economic Papers*, vol. 18, pp. 284–8.
BLAUG, M. (1968) *Economic Theory in Retrospect*, Heinemann, London.
BRUNI, F. (1978) 'Appunti sulla teoria monetaria di Knut Wicksell', *Giornale degli Economisti e Annali di Economia*, Settembre-Ottobre, pp. 579–629.
BRUSCO, S. (1976) 'Introduction' to the Italian edition of Wicksell, 1893, Isedi, Milano, pp. ix–xl.
CASSEL, G. (1922) *Money and Foreign Exchanges After 1914*, London.
CASSEL, G. (1932) *The Theory of Social Economy*, vol. II, Ernest Benn Limited, London.
CHIODI, G. (1978) 'Some Reflections on Marx, Sraffa and the Theory of Distribution', *Science and Society*, vol. XLII, pp. 33–42.
CHIODI, G. (1978–9) 'Appunti per una generalizzazione della teoria monetaria di Wicksell', *Quaderni di Economia*, Annali della Facoltà di Scienze Politiche, Perugia, pp. 29–38.
CLOWER, R. (1965) 'The Keynesian Counterrevolution: A Theoretical Appraisal', in F. H. Hahn and F. P. R. Brechling (eds), *The Theory of Interest Rates*, Macmillan & Co. Ltd, London, pp. 103–25.
CONARD, J. W. (1959) *An Introduction to the Theory of Interest*, University of California Press, Berkeley and Los Angeles.
DE CECCO, M. (1974) *Money and Empire*, Basil Blackwell, Oxford.
DEHEM, R. (1957) 'Swedish Economic Policy and Thinking', *Canadian Journal of Economics and Political Science*, August, pp. 416–30.
DESAI, M. (n.d.) *The Task of Monetary Theory: The Hayek–Sraffa Debate in a Modern Perspective*, Institut des Sciences Economiques, Louvain-La-Neuve, mimeo.
DI GASPARE, S. (1979) *Moneta-Segno o Moneta-Merce. Studio sulla teoria monetaria di Wicksell e Marx*, G. Giappichelli Editore, Torino.
FRISCH, R. (1935–6) 'On the Notion of Equilibrium and Disequilibrium', *Review of Economic Studies*, pp. 100–5.
FRISCH, R. (1952) 'Frisch on Wicksell', in H. W. Spiegel (ed.), *The Development of Economic Thought. Great Economists in Perspective*, John Wiley & Sons, Inc., New York; Chapman & Hale, Ltd, London.
GÅRDLUND, T. (1958) *The Life of Knut Wicksell*, Almqvist & Wicksell, Stockholm.

Bibliography 123

GAREGNANI, P. (1960) *Il capitale nelle teorie della distribuzione*, Giuffrè, Milano.

GAREGNANI, P. (1979) 'Notes on Consumption, Investment and Effective Demand: II', *Cambridge Journal of Economics*, March, 1979, pp. 63–82. (Originally published in 1965.)

GUSTAFSSON, B. (1973) 'A Perennial of Doctrinal History: Keynes and "The Stockholm School"', *Economics and History*, vol. XVI, pp. 114–28.

HAAVELMO, T. (1978) 'Wicksell on the Currency Theory vs. the Banking Principle', *Scandinavian Journal of Economics*, vol. 80, n. 2, pp. 209–15.

HAHN, F. H. (1973) *On the Notion of Equilibrium in Economics*, Cambridge University Press, London.

HAMILTON, C. (1979) 'Expectations and the Stockholm School', *Scandinavian Journal of Economics*, pp. 434–9.

HAMMARSKJÖLD, D. (1955) 'The Swedish Discussion on the Aims of Monetary Policy', *International Economic Papers*, n. 5, pp. 145–54.

HAYEK, F. A. (1931) *Prices and Production*, George Routledge & Sons, Ltd, London.

HECKSCHER, E. F. (1952) 'David Davidson', *International Economic Papers*, n. 2, pp. 112–35.

HECKSCHER, E. F. (1953) 'A Survey of Economic Thought in Sweden, 1875–1950', *Scandinavian Economic History Review*, vol. I, n. 1, pp. 105–25.

HICKS, J. R. (1946) *Value and Capital*, 2nd edn, Oxford University Press, London.

HICKS, J. R. (1965) *Capital and Growth*, Oxford University Press, London.

HICKS, J. R. (1977) *Economic Perspectives. Further Essays on Money and Growth*, Oxford University Press, London.

HUGHES, J. R. T. (1968) 'Wicksell on the Facts: Prices and Interest Rates, 1844 to 1914', in J. N. Wolfe (ed.), *Value, Capital and Growth*, Paper in honour of Sir John Hicks, Edinburgh University Press, pp. 215–55.

HUME, D. (1963) 'Of Interest', in D. Hume, *Essays – Moral, Political and Literary*, Oxford University Press, London, pp. 303–15. (Originally published in 1752.)

HUMPHREY, T. M. (1976) 'Interest Rates, Expectation, and the Wicksellian Policy Rule', *Atlanta Economic Journal*, vol. IV, n. 1, pp. 9–20.

JONUNG, L. (1981) 'Ricardo on Machinery and the Present Unemployment: An Unpublished Manuscript by Knut Wicksell', *Economic Journal*, March, pp. 195–205.

KEYNES, J. M. (1916) Letter to Wicksell, dated 26 June 1916. (This letter, as well as the others listed below, can be found in the Archives of the Central Library of Lund University, Sweden.)

KEYNES, J. M. (1930) *A Treatise on Money. The Pure Theory of Money*, published in 1971 as vol. V of *The Collected Writings of John Maynard Keynes*, Macmillan St. Martin's Press, London.

KEYNES, J. M. (1936) *The General Theory of Employment Interest and Money*, Macmillan St. Martin's Press, London.

KNUDTZON, E. J. (1976) *Knut Wicksell Tryckta skrifter 1868–1950*, (The publications of Knut Wicksell 1868–1950) CWK Gleerup, Lund.

LAIDLER, D. (1972) 'On Wicksell Theory of Price Level Dynamics', *The Manchester School of Economic and Social Studies*, vol. 41 (4), pp. 125–44.
LANDGREN, K. G. (1957) *Economics in Modern Sweden*, Library of Congress, Reference Department, Washington.
LAWSON, T. (1981) 'Keynesian Model Building and the Rational Expectations Critique', *Cambridge Journal of Economics*, December, pp. 311–26.
LEIJONHUFVUD, A. (1968) *On Keynesian Economics and the Economics of Keynes*, Oxford University Press, New York.
LEIJONHUFVUD, A. (1969) 'Keynes and the Keynesians: A Suggested Interpretation', in R. W. Clower (ed.), *Monetary Theory*, Richard Clay Ltd, Bungay, Suffolk, pp. 298–310. (Originally published in 1967.)
LEIJONHUFVUD, A. (1981) 'The Wicksell Connection, Variations on a Theme', in A. Leijonhufvud (ed.), *Information and Coordination: Essays in Macroeconomic Theory*, Oxford University Press, London, pp. 131–202.
LERNER, A. (1952) 'The Essential Properties of Interest and Money', *Quarterly Journal of Economics*, May, pp. 172–93.
LERNER, A. (1953) 'Some Swedish Stepping Stones in Economic Theory', in A. Lerner, *Essays in Economic Analysis*, Macmillan & Co. Ltd, London, pp. 215–41.
LINDAHL, E. (1939) *Studies in the Theory of Money and Capital*, George Allen & Unwin Ltd, London.
LINDAHL, E. (ed.) (1969) *Knut Wicksell – Selected Papers on Economic Theory*, August M. Kelley, New York.
MARGET, A. W. (1966) *The Theory of Prices*, vol. II, Augustus M. Kelley, New York. (Originally published in 1942.)
MARSCHAK, J. (1941) 'Wicksell's Two Interest Rates', *Social Research*, November, pp. 469–78.
MARX, K. (1973) *Grundisse*, translated with a Foreword by M. Nicolaus, Penguin Books Ltd, Harmondsworth, Middlesex. (Written in 1857–8 and originally published in 1939–41.)
MARX, K. (1974) *Capital*, vol. I, Lawrence & Wishart, London. (Originally published in 1867.)
MARX, K. (1972) *Capital*, vol. III, Lawrence & Wishart, London. (Written in 1864–5 and originally published in 1894.)
MASSIE, J. (1750) *An Essay on the Governing Causes of the Natural Rate of Interest*, W. Owen, London.
METZLER, L. A. (1950) 'The Rate of Interest and the Marginal Product of Capital', *Journal of Political Economy*, August, pp. 289–306.
MISES, L. von (1934) *The Theory of Money and Credit*, Jonathan Cape, London.
MYRDAL, G. (1939) *Monetary Equilibrium*, William Hodge & Company, Glasgow. (Originally published in 1931.)
OHLIN, B. (1926) 'Obituary – Knut Wicksell (1851–1926)', *Economic Journal*, September, pp. 503–12.
OHLIN, B. (1936) 'Introduction' to K. Wicksell, 1898b, Macmillan & Co., London, pp. vii–xxi.
OHLIN, B. (1937a) 'Some Notes on the Stockholm Theory of Savings and

Investment, I', *Economic Journal*, March, pp. 53–69.
OHLIN, B. (1937b) 'Some Notes on the Stockholm Theory of Savings and Investment, II', *Economic Journal*, June, pp. 221–40.
OHLIN, B. (1960) 'The Stockholm School Versus the Quantity Theory', *International Economic Papers*, n. 10, pp. 132–46.
OHLIN, B. (1977) 'Some Comments on Keynesianism and the Swedish Theory of Expansion before 1935', in D. Patinkin and J. C. Leith (eds), *Keynes, Cambridge and 'The General Theory'*, Macmillan, London.
OHLIN, B. (1978) 'On the Formulation of Monetary Theory', *History of Political Economy*, 10:3, pp. 353–88. (Originally published in 1933.)
PALANDER, T. (1953) 'Some Methodological Reflections on Myrdal's "Monetary Equilibrium"', *International Economic Papers*, n. 3, pp. 5–57.
PANICO, C. (1980) 'Marx's Analysis of the Relationship between the Rate of Interest and the Rate of Profits', *Cambridge Journal of Economics*, December, pp. 363–78.
PASINETTI, L. L. (1980–81) 'The Rate of Interest and the Distribution of Income in a Pure Labor Economy', *Journal of Post Keynesian Economics*, Winter, pp. 170–82.
PATINKIN, D. (1965) *Money, Interest, and Prices*, 2nd edn, Harper & Row, New York.
PATINKIN, D. (1968) 'Wicksell's Cumulative Process in Theory and Practice', *Banca Nazionale del Lavoro, Quarterly Review*, June, pp. 120–31.
PATINKIN, D. (1978) 'Some Observations on Ohlin's 1933 Article', *History of Political Economy*, 10:3, pp. 413–19.
RICARDO, D. (1951a) *On the Principle of Political Economy and Taxation*, vol. I of *The Works and Correspondence of David Ricardo*, edited by Piero Sraffa with the collaboration of M. H. Dobb, Cambridge University Press, London. (1st edn originally published in 1817.)
RICARDO, D. (1951b) *Pamphlets and Papers 1809–1811*, vol. III, of *The Works and Correspondence of David Ricardo*, edited by Piero Sraffa with the collaboration of M. H. Dobb, Cambridge University Press, London.
RIST, C. (1940) *History of Monetary and Credit Theory*, George Allen & Unwin, London. (Originally published in 1938.)
SANGER, C. P. (1898) 'Review' of K. Wicksell 1898b, *The Economic Journal*, vol. 8, pp. 384–6.
SAUERBECK, A. (1895) 'Index Number of Prices', *Economic Journal*, June, pp. 161–74.
SAYERS, R. S. (1953) 'Ricardo's Views on Monetary Questions', in T. S. Ashton and R. S. Sayers (eds), *Papers in English Monetary History*, Oxford University Press, London, pp. 76–95.
SCANAGATTA, G. (1978) 'Tassi degli interessi, credito bancario e livello dei prezzi', *Rivista bancaria*, March–April, pp. 133–41.
SCHUMPETER, J. A. (1954) *History of Economic Analysis*, George Allen & Unwin Ltd, London.
SELIGMAN, E. R. A. (1910) Letter to Wicksell, dated 14 October 1910.
SHACKLE, G. L. S. (1967) *The Years of High Theory*, Cambridge University Press, London.
SRAFFA, P. (1925) 'Sulle relazioni tra costo e quantità prodotta', *Annali di Economia*, pp. 277–328.

SRAFFA, P. (1926) 'The Laws of Returns under Competitive Conditions', *Economic Journal*, vol. XXXVI, pp. 535–50.

SRAFFA, P. (1932) 'Dr. Hayek on Money and Capital', *Economic Journal*, March, pp. 42–51.

SRAFFA, P. (1960) *Production of Commodities By Means of Commodities*, C. U. P., Cambridge.

STEIGER, O. (1976) 'Bertil Ohlin and the Origins of the Keynesian Revolution', *History of Political Economy*, 8:3, pp. 341–66.

STEIGER, O. (1978) 'Prelude to the Theory of a Monetary Economy: Origins and Significance of Ohlin's 1933 Approach', *History of Political Economy*, 10:3, pp. 420–46.

TAUSSIG, F. W. (1914) Letter to Wicksell, dated 7 January 1914.

THALBERG, B. (1979) 'Introduction' to two unpublished papers of Wicksell, in S. Steinar and B. Thalberg (eds), *The Theoretical Contributions of Knut Wicksell*, The Macmillan Press Ltd, London and Basingstoke, pp. 103–51.

THOMAS, B. (1935) 'The Monetary Doctrines of Professor Davidson', *Economic Journal*, March, pp. 36–50.

THOMAS, B. (1936) 'Swedish Monetary Theory since Wicksell', in B. Thomas, *Monetary, Policy and Crises*, George Routledge & Sons Ltd, London, pp. 62–108.

THORNTON, H. (1939) *An Inquiry into the Nature and Effects of the Paper Credit of Great Britain*, edited with an introduction by F. A. von Hayek, George Allen & Unwin Ltd, London. (Originally published in 1802.)

TOOKE, T. (1844) *An Inquiry into the Currency Principle*, Longman, Brown, Green & Longmans, London.

UHR, C. G. (1951) 'Knut Wicksell – A Centennial Evaluation', *The American Economic Review*, December, pp. 829–60.

UHR, C. G. (1960) *Economic Doctrines of Knut Wicksell*, University of California Press, Berkeley and Los Angeles.

UHR, C. G. (1975) *Economic Doctrines of David Davidson*, Uppsala.

VINER, J. (1965) *Studies in the Theory of International Trade*, Augustus M. Kelley, Clifton. (Originally published in 1937.)

WALRAS, L. (1886) *Theorie de la monnaie*, Imprimerie Corbaz & Cie, Lausanne.

WALRAS, L. (1954) *Elements of Pure Economics*, translated by W. Jaffé, George Allen & Unwin Ltd, London. (Originally published in 1874.)

WICKSELL, K. (1893) *Über Wert, Kapital und Rente nach den neueren nationalökonomischen Theorien*, Verlag von Gustav Fischer, Jena. (Translated by S. H. Frowein as *Value, Capital and Rent*, George Allen & Unwin Ltd, London, 1954.)

WICKSELL, K. (1896) *Finanztheoretische Untersuchungen nebst Darstellung und Kritik des Steuerweses Schwedens*, Verlag von Gustav Fischer, Jena.

WICKSELL, K. (1897) 'Der Bankzins als Regulator der Warenpreise', *Jahrbücher für Nationalökonomie und Statistik*, 68, pp. 228–43.

WICKSELL, K. (1898a) 'Penningräntans inflytande på varuprisen', in *Nationalekonomiska föreningens-sammanträde den 14 April 1898*, Stockholm, 1899, pp. 1–26. (Translated by Sylva Gethin as 'The Influence of the Rate

of Interest on Commodity Prices', in Lindahl (ed.) (1969), pp. 67–89.)
WICKSELL, K. (1898b) *Geldzins und Güterpreise, Eine Studie über die den Tauschwert des Geldes bestimmenden Ursachen*, Verlag von Gustav Fischer, Jena. (Translated by R. F. Kahn as *Interest and Prices*, Macmillan & Co., London, 1936.)
WICKSELL, K. (1901) *Föreläsningar i Nationalekonomi*, Första delen: Teoretisk Nationalekonomi, Lund. (Translated by E. Classen as *Lectures on Political Economy*, vol. I, The Macmillan Company, New York, 1935.)
WICKSELL, K. (1906) *Föreläsningar i Nationalekonomi*, Andra delen: Om Penningar och Kredit, Stockholm, (Translated by E. Classen as *Lectures on Political Economy*, vol. II, The Macmillan Company, New York, 1935.)
WICKSELL, K. (1907a) 'The Influence of the Rate of Interest on Prices', *The Economic Journal*, June, pp. 213–20.
WICKSELL, K. (1907b) 'Krisernas gåta', *Statskønomisk Tidsskrift*, pp. 255–84. (Translated by C. G. Uhr as 'The Enigma of Business Cycle', *International Economic Papers*, vol. 3, 1953, pp. 58–75.)
WICKSELL, K. (1908) Letter to Umberto Ricci, dated 17 July 1908.
WICKSELL, K. (1910) Letter to Edwin R. A. Seligman, dated 22 September 1910.
WICKSELL, K. (1919) 'Professor Cassels nationalekonomiska system', *Ekonomisk Tidsskrift*, pp. 195–226. (Translated by S. Alder, as an Appendix to the English edn of Wicksell (1901), pp. 219–57.)
WICKSELL, K. (1925) 'Valutaspörsmålet i de skandinaviska länderna', *Ekonomisk Tidsskrift*, pp. 205–22. (Translated by H. Norberg as 'The Monetary Problem of the Scandinavian Countries', Appendix to the English edn of Wicksell (1898b) pp. 199–219.) N. B. A complete list of Wicksell's works can be found in Knudtzon (1976).
WINCH, D. (1966) 'The Keynesian Revolution in Sweden', *Journal of Political Economy*, April, pp. 168–76.
YOHE, W. P. (1978) 'Ohlin's 1933 Reformation of Monetary Theory', *History of Political Economy*, 10:3, pp. 447–53.

Index of Names

Adarkar, B. P. 38n
Åkerman, J. 13n

Bailey, R. E. 54
Bhaduri, A. 61n
Blaug, M. 47
Böhm-Bawerk, E. 48
Bosanquet, C. 24
Bruni, F. 86n
Brusco, S. 61

Cassel, G. 38, 116, 117, 119
Chiodi, G. xiin
Clower, R. 66
Conard, J. W. 24

Davidson, D. 114, 121n
De Cecco, M. 13n
Dehem, R. 103n
Desai, M. 38
Di Gaspare, S. xi, 13n
Ditta, L. xi

Frisch, R. xiin, 38n, 47n

Gårdlund, T. xiin, 48, 121n
Garegnani, P. 61n, 84n
Gibson, A. H. 90
Graziani, A. xi
Gustafsson, B. 103n

Haavelmo, T. 13n
Hahn, F. H. 85n, 93n
Hamilton, C. 103n
Hammarskjöld, D. 103n
Hayek, F. xi, 24, 47, 84n
Heckscher, E. F. 103n, 121n
Hicks, J. R. 8, 94, 95, 96, 97, 98, 99, 100, 101, 102, 103, 103n, 104, 109
Hughes, J. R. T. 61n
Hume, D. 4
Humphrey, T. M. 54

Kahn, R. 113
Keynes, J. M. ix, 24, 37n, 61n, 104, 113, 121n

Laidler, D. 54
Langreen, K. G. 103n

Lawson, T. 61n
Leijonhufvud, A. 37n, 66, 92n, 93n
Lerner, A. P. 24, 103n
Lindahl, E. ix, xiin, 97, 104, 105, 106, 107, 108, 109, 113

Marcuzzo, M. C. xi
Marget, A. W. 13n
Marschak, J. 86n
Marshall, A. 54, 85n
Marx, K. 31, 37n, 38n, 45, 90
Massie, J. 37n
Meldolesi, L. xi
Messori, M. xi
Metzler, L. A. 61n
Mises, L. 38n
Myrdal, G. ix, 104, 109, 110, 112, 113, 121n

Nasse, E. 45

Ohlin, B. 44, 60, 61, 103n, 104, 113, 114, 115, 117, 119, 120

Palander, T. 103n
Panico, C. 37n
Pascal, B. 77
Pasinetti, L. L. 38n
Patinkin, D. 13n, 62, 64, 65, 66, 67, 68, 69, 70, 71, 72, 73, 74, 75, 76, 77, 79, 80, 84n, 85n, 90, 91, 92, 94, 95, 102, 103n, 107
Pigou, A. C. 85n

Ricardo, D. x, 1, 2, 3, 6, 7, 8, 9, 10, 11, 12, 13n, 48, 49, 79, 85n, 103n
Ricci, U. 86n
Rist, C. 7

Sanger, C. P. 47
Sauerbeck, A. 51
Say, J. B. 44, 84
Sayers, R. S. 13n
Scanagatta, G. 86n
Schumpeter, J. A. 38n, 119
Seligman, E. R. 121n
Shackle, G. L. S. 103n
Sraffa, P. ix, xi, 13n, 24, 38n, 47, 59, 84n, 88, 99, 120, 121n

128

Steiger, O.   103n

Taussig, F. W.   121n
Thalberg, B.   xi
Thomas, B.   121n
Thornton, H.   37n
Tooke, T.   6, 51, 53, 57, 61n

Uhr, C. G.   54, 121n

Velupillai, K.   viii, xi

Vercelli, A.   xi
Viner, J.   7

Walras, L.   49, 65, 69, 85n
Webb, U.   109
Wicksell, K.   *passim*
Winch, D.   103n

Yohe, W. P.   103n

Guglielmo Chiodi is Professor of Political Economy at the University of Perugia, Italy. After graduating at the University of Rome, he engaged in research work at the University of Cambridge. He has been Visiting Scholar at the Wicksell Archives of the University of Lund and a Visiting Professor at the European University of Florence. He is the author of books and professional articles in the areas of value and distribution, and monetary theory.